PERMISSION GRANTED.

TAKE IT ALL BACK

This book is dedicated to

Jesus Christ and His finished work on the Cross

To devout believers in the Lord, whose human doubt, dismay, and disbelief demands and necessitates the Cross of Christ and the grace of God

To sincere followers of Jesus Christ, who have made up their minds to follow Him and leave the world behind

To active Sunday morning worshippers who desire a deeper, more meaningful understanding of God's Word on a daily basis

To inactive church members around the world who peeped into the window of a local assembly of Christians and found liberalism, legalism, religious hypocrisy, and not God's redemptive love

To pastors who have been called by the Lord of the Cross to preach the Gospel but have somehow missed preaching, teaching, and sharing the truth regarding the subject of restoration

To every real Christian who can say, "I love the Lord with everything in me, and yet, I still struggle from time to time while under the sanctified reconstruction of the Lord."

PERMISSION GRANTED:

TAKE IT ALL BACK

RECOVERED ITEMS:
PEACE, JOY, MIND, HEALTH, FAMILY

Dr John R. Adolph

Library of Congress Catalog Number: 2025947756

Name:	Adolph, John R., Author
Title:	*Permission Granted: Restoration and Reclamation from a Biblical Perspective*
	John R. Adolph
	Advantage Books, 2025
Identifiers:	ISBN Paperback: 9781597558549
	ISBN eBook: 9781597558686
Subjects:	Books › Religion & Spirituality › Worship & Devotion Devotionals
	Books › Religion & Spirituality › Worship & Devotion Inspirational
	Books › Religion & Spirituality › Worship & Devotion Prayer

First Printing: October 2025
25 26 27 28 29 30 31   10 9 8 7 6 5 4 3 2 1

Table of Contents

ACKNOWLEDGEMENTS

Each time I have been blessed to pen another literary work, I am reminded of just how important it is to be inspired by the Lord and surrounded by people who have been placed by Him to help it come to fruition. With this in mind, the book you now hold in your hand is not the solo work of the name found on the front cover. This work is the result of the love, labor, toil, time, sacrifice, and servitude of a multitude of people who cause works like this one to develop.

With this in mind, I want to thank the Lord for the person of the Holy Ghost, who has been my true inspiration for every book I have ever written. He speaks to the still quiet portals of my soul in ways that I can hear Him and obey.

I have to say thank you, Jesus, for the fragrant flower of my family and the Antioch Baptist Church fellowship, my wonderful, faithful wife of thirty years, Lady Dorrie Adolph. I sincerely appreciate the prayers you pray, the patience you exude, the love you exhibit, and the grace-filled partnership you provide that holds our family together. I also want to thank God for my two wonderful children, Sumone and Jonathan, whose walk with Jesus Christ as young adults has inspired me greatly. To my precious immediate family whose prayers keep me going: Pastor Seymour (Sonny) and Karen Adolph, Daisy (Nell) and Curtis Barlow, Ron and Wandy Adolph, and Pastor Vincent and Tina Washington.

I appreciate the relentless excellence of my Executive Director and CAO, Minister Brooklyn Williams, for her desire to see God use me to the fullest. I also celebrate the faithful support of my Chief Executive Staff, who are the real game changers in all that the Lord has assigned to my hands: Dr. Karen Davis, CMO; Rev. Jamison Malbrough, Youth Pastor; and Sister Felicia Young, CFO and Global Missions Coordinator.

I praise God for the servant leaders of the Antioch Church family who partner with me in kingdom building endeavors in the person of Deacon Dale Boudreaux and the Deacons Ministry; Deacon Norris Bennett and the Trustee Ministry; Deacon Arthur Louis,

Treasurer, Pastor Roger Shillow and the Clergy Ministry and Church Officers who labor tirelessly ministering to the body of Christ so that I can have the time needed to produce Discipleship material for our church family to use.

I must personally applaud the matchless diligence of my day staff at Antioch who work on the front line of the battle every day in the persons of Pastor Albert Moore, Minister Kim Hardy, Sister Deandra Darby, Minister Linda Jones, Deacon Gregory Griffin, and Deacon Reggie Wasson.

I honor the presence of my senior-most day staff who have labored at my side through every moment of my ministry in Beaumont, Texas, for nearly three decades: Rev. Major M. Goldman, III, Sister Jewel "Sue" Cooper, Pastor Jack Gay, and Sister Lorraine Lemons (recently retired).

I'm humbled by the toil, time, and labor of my graphic designer, transcriber, editor, and publisher, who are responsible for taking my scattered notes and thoughts and causing them to become the work that you now hold in your hand. With this at heart, I'm forever indebted to Rev. Alfred Beverly, Brother Landon Richard, Sister Lori Ceasar, Dr. Porchanee' White, and Brother Mike Janiczek, respectively.

Most importantly, I have to say thank you, Jesus, for the marvelous members of the Antioch Church who listen to sermon after sermon and read book after book as we seek to fulfill the three Core Values of the Lord's Church that we sincerely believe in: the Great Commission, the Great Commandment, and the Great Calling.

PREFACE

Have you ever been devastated? Depleted? Disoriented? Truth is, the challenges of life often move us to that point. When life has worn us down and stressed us out, we are often tempted of the enemy to "tuck tail and run"!

Not so with the worshiper and warrior David, who after experiencing devastation, depletion and disorientation decided he would not let that trio of trauma get the last word. This amazing work by my friend and brother, Dr. John Robert Adolph, shares practical principles of recovery and renewal when we learn that in many of these seasons of life, we have been granted permission to bounce back and recover all that has been lost!

I have been abundantly blessed by a 30-year friendship with John Adolph. His insight and intellect have amazed me each time I have been blessed to glean from his ministry. His dogged passion fuels his divine purpose to educate and empower God's people to become the committed disciples we have been destined to become and to live out our faith in ways that engender victorious lifestyles.

Consequently, I am delighted that Adolph's twentieth published work invites us to *take it all back!* His admonishment emanates from 1 Samuel 30:8, when the worshiper David seeks the Lord for the opportunity to retrieve all that his enemies had raided from their camp—most importantly, their families! The Lord, in essence, says, ***Permission Granted***, and consequently, the warrior David recovers all! These next pages inspire and instruct us to do the same in the various areas of our lives where we have experienced devastation, depletion and disorientation.

I am so glad my brother has not forgotten about those of us who need to experience his brilliance in print. As you read this work, may God grant you the permission to take back all that has caused you lack and loss throughout the years.

Thank God for the ministry of Dr. John R. Adolph!

Marcus D. Cosby
Senior Pastor, Wheeler Avenue Baptist Church, Houston, Texas

FOREWORD

Dr. John R. Adolph has taken up the proverbial pen (or fingers to the keyboard) to offer readers this reflection on 1 Samuel 30:1-10, providing insights and inspiration for dealing with loss and recovery. The story of David and the place called Ziklag remains relevant today, as many African Americans and other marginalized groups face loss due to partisan politics, corrupt economics, shifting societal morals, and distorted spiritualities. People are being robbed of their dignity and destiny, which hampers their ability to exercise agency over their identity—an identity connected to the Creator God through Jesus Christ by the power of the Holy Spirit. The Trinitarian God calls to battle and grants permission to recover what has been stolen.

Yet, recovery carries an undertone of resistance to the status quo and defiance of evil. If one engages in recovery, which the Divine has granted permission for, it shows that it requires effort and struggle on our part. While Yahweh grants permission, we must be willing to do the work of struggle and resistance to reclaim what was once ours. Dr. Adolph poignantly and pastorally conceives biblical strategies and confronts internal and external enemies to recover precious people and vital artifacts, making us whole.
This story of David at Ziklag highlights resilience, recovery, restitution, and restoration due to David's personal assessment and empowerment. Through internal encouragement and seeking divine permission, David set his ambition like flint, driven by godly tenacity to pursue what was rightfully his.

Dr. Adolph empowers the reader to rise from the ashes of apathy and the mud of mediocrity to reclaim what was once ours: dignity, respect, identity, and power. He informs us that Ziklag is not just David's battlefield; it is our battleground. We are called not to be passive, but to fight for what is ours, what is right, what is just, and what is fair. Tears will fall. Blood will be shed. Scars will form. Yet, they will serve as reminders of how to confront corrupt systems, fractured families, cowardly leaders, and fickle supporters in the pursuit of what God has declared belongs to YOU.

Dr. Adolph reminds us of the God who grants permission to pursue, overtake, and recover all. As you read this pastoral and prophetic opus, know that God has granted you permission to engage in recovery for your existential reality and ontological being. This is a message for those who are tired of crying and sighing. God can give you beauty for ashes and turn your mourning into dancing. Let your soul be inspired by this timely message. May you go and receive what God has for you. Dr. Adolph informs us that permission has been granted.

Reverend Dr. Robert Charles Scott
Senior Pastor, St. Paul Baptist Church, Charlotte, NC
VP Hampton University Ministers Conference
2nd VP Lott Carey Foreign Mission Convention

INTRODUCTION

To be clear, nowhere in the Bible does God give believers a direct command to go and take back anything that the enemy has stolen. However, the Lord definitely permits, empowers, orchestrates, and allows believers the benefit to recover what the enemy has stolen that he thinks he can keep. The raison d'être of this work rests within the confines of this argument.

Please make no mistake about it, our enemy has a set agenda. The mission statement of the devil is to be "a thief that comes to steal, kill and destroy..." (St. John 10:10a, KJV). In this stead, we should never be shocked or surprised when our adversary does what our Lord told us He would do. In a sincere and devout sense, if you are a Christian who loves God, you should anticipate satanic setbacks and demon-filled distractions to come your way.

In the book of 1 Samuel 30:1-10, King David encounters a severe attack by the enemy. Here is how the passage reads,

And it came to pass, when David and his men were come to Ziklag on the third day, that the Amalekites had invaded the south, and Ziklag, and smitten Ziklag, and burned it with fire; ² And had taken the women captives, that were therein: they slew not any, either great or small, but carried them away, and went on their way. ³ So David and his men came to the city, and, behold, it was burned with fire; and their wives, and their sons, and their daughters, were taken captives. ⁴ Then David and the people that were with him lifted up their voice and wept, until they had no more power to weep. 5 And David's two wives were taken captives, Ahinoam the Jezreelitess, and Abigail the wife of Nabal the Carmelite. ⁶ And David was greatly distressed; for the people spake of stoning him, because the soul of all the people was grieved, every man for his sons and for his daughters: but David encouraged himself in the Lord his God. ⁷ And David said to Abiathar the priest, Ahimelech's son, I pray thee, bring me hither the ephod. And Abiathar brought thither the ephod to David. ⁸ And David inquired at the Lord, saying, Shall I pursue after this troop? shall I overtake them? And he answered him, Pursue: for thou shalt surely overtake them, and without fail recover all. 9 So David went, he and the six hundred men that were with him, and came to the brook Besor, where those that were left behind stayed. [10] But David pursued, he and four hundred men: for two hundred abode behind, which were so faint that they could not go over the brook Besor. ([1 Samuel 30:1–10](#), KJV).

This attack is so horrid that David's men and community had open talks about putting him to death as their leader. However, King David "...encouraged himself in the Lord his God" (vs. 6). The Amalekites have taken their women and children hostage and burned the entire town. With a city that has been torched and men who have their doubts, David finds his way to the lap of God and asks the Lord if he can pursue his enemy, and the Lord gives him the green light. It is with this pericope in mind that this book finds its canonical core.

Even though the enemy had attacked David, he did not go after them until the Lord of heaven permitted him to do so. Did you hear that? God gave David permission to go and take back what the enemy had stolen.

With this passage in mind, it should be noted that the same God who permitted King David to take it all back has also extended to every believer in the Lord Jesus Christ a similar grace. For the next fifteen weeks, you will take a journey through the Bible and consider things that the enemy is known for stealing, with the permission of God, for you to take it back! Each week, you will be presented with a theme for the week, a concrete Word from the Lord that you should really meditate on for the day, a mandate given by God from the scriptures, a message regarding the mandate, and a mission statement that embraces the personal application of the Word that has been shared. Each week, you will close with a prayer of meditation and an action element called ***"Permission Granted"*** that will involve you putting your faith into action and taking back what the enemy has stolen from you.

Prepare yourself to be blessed, empowered, informed, enlightened, and encouraged through this devotional study you are about to take. Most importantly, before you start this fifteen-week journey, establish a set place and time that you will meet the Lord each day for the purpose of study and prayer, if you do not already have one.

As you read each devotional entry, you will notice the interchangeable usage of pronouns and possessive determiners such as: I, me, my, we, us, and our. This is intentional and placed for the purpose of highlighting the fact that none of us as Christians take our journey through life alone. Most importantly, each devotional exercise takes about four minutes to complete. Think about this for a moment: there are twenty-four hours in a day, giving you one thousand four hundred and forty minutes that you can use daily. God is worthy of just four minutes of the time He is giving you each day. This is a nice way of saying, "make some time for God," as you plan to read this devotional. There are some things the enemy has that belong to you, and through the teaching that you will discover in this devotional guide, you will, with God's permission, take it all back!

Day 1

God's Word For You Today:

THE DEVIL MAY HAVE IT, BUT IT DOESN'T MEAN THAT HE CAN KEEP IT

The Mandate

And David enquired at the LORD, saying, Shall I pursue after this troop? shall I overtake them? And He answered him, Pursue: for thou shalt surely overtake them, and without fail recover all (1 Samuel 30:8, KJV).

The Message

In our study passage for this week, David faces some bad actors who are well known for violence and corruption, called the Amalekites. They have invaded Ziklag and burned it with fire. They have kidnapped their women and left town. It was so bad that David's men and community thought about killing him. But David took courage in the Lord (vs. 5). And God empowered the King to go and take everything back that the Amalekites had that belonged to him (vs. 8).

The Mission

Just as the Lord of Hosts gave David permission to go and take back what the Amalekites had taken, He has granted the same permission to you. Just as David reclaimed what was His by right, so can you! The key faith factor in this passage is understanding that David asked the Lord if he could pursue the enemy to take back what had been stolen from him, and God gave him permission. As you read today's devotional lesson, I encourage you to do what David did. Your permission has been granted!

The Meditation

Lord, I have lived long enough to know that the devil is a thief and a liar. I refuse to let him have anything You died for me to keep. With Your spirit living within me and Your favor resting upon me, I will prayerfully fight to take back what the enemy thinks he can keep. Thank You for the victory over the enemy!

In The Name of Jesus, Amen.

Day 2

God's Word For You Today:

YOU NEED CLEARANCE TO DO THAT

The Mandate

And David enquired at the LORD, saying, Shall I pursue after this troop? shall I overtake them? And he answered him, Pursue: for thou shalt surely overtake them, and without fail recover all (1 Samuel 30:8, KJV).

The Message

When you read this passage carefully, you will notice that David does not just go after the enemy. Neither does he demand the return of his loved ones. The first thing he does is, "David enquired at the Lord". This is critical to understanding the truth of what took place. Look closely at the passage above. David asks two questions: "shall I pursue them? Shall I overtake them?" The humility and dependency expressed in this passage says, "God, I cannot do anything like this without You!"

The Mission

Jesus told His disciples that they could not do anything without Him (St. John 15:5, KJV). The point here is to always seek God in whatever you do. Just because you think it is a good idea does not mean it is a God idea or something that He wants you to do. To do anything without God's help means you are defeated before you ever get started.

The Meditation

Eternal God in heaven, I want You to know that I realize without You I can do nothing, but with You I can do all things. Thank You, Lord, for victory in the face of defeat. Your presence in my life is the difference maker.

In The Name of Jesus, Amen.

Day 3

God's Word For You Today:

SOME ANSWERED PRAYERS MAKE YOU PRAISE GOD

The Mandate

And David enquired at the LORD, saying, Shall I pursue after this troop? shall I overtake them? And he answered him, Pursue: for thou shalt surely overtake them, and without fail recover all (1 Samuel 30:8, KJV).

The Message

The answered prayer of this passage is enough to cause anyone to desire to praise God. It is easy to thank God when He says yes to you. Yes to your health being healed, yes to your increase and to your overflow, or yes to a promotion on your job or a new door of opportunity. It is always more difficult to say thank you when God says no. In today's passage, the Lord tells David, ' Yes. '

The Mission

When God says yes, do not doubt it. Receive the answer of yes as if it has already taken place. God's 'yes' for you today is as fresh as bread out of the oven. It is as solid as a rock or a boulder. If God says yes, believe Him, and let that be the settlement of all you need to move forward.

The Meditation

And so, God, today I want you to know that I trust your answer of 'yes' as if my victory had already taken place. I celebrate Your power, Your sovereignty, Your ubiquity, and Your strength. Thank You for the victory today.

In The Name of Jesus, Amen.

Day 4

God's Word For You Today:

GOD WILL MAKE A WAY SOMEHOW

The Mandate
And David enquired at the LORD, saying, Shall I pursue after this troop? shall I overtake them? And he answered him, Pursue: for thou shalt surely overtake them, and without fail recover all (1 Samuel 30:8, KJV).

The Message
When David pursues the Lord in prayer and receives an answer of yes regarding whether he should go and fight for his family, something amazing takes place. God does not tell him how He would give him victory over the Amalekites and return his family to him. The great news of the day is that God did it. Oftentimes in scripture, the how-to of the will of God is very unclear. In short, by faith, you learn a valuable lesson as it relates to walking with God, which is that the Lord will make a way somehow.

The Mission
The Lord's way is never your way. It is never our way. It is never an easy way. It is never, ever what we think it should be. God's way is mysterious. He works things out the way He wants them worked out, only for you to make sure that when you gain the victory, you must give the glory to Him. In this story, the glory belongs to God because David gets back what the enemy has taken from him. Just like God did it for David, He can do the same thing for you.

The Meditation
Today, Lord, my prayer unto You is for You to work it out the way You want to work it out. God, I will obey You. I will do exactly what You've commanded me to do, and I will make sure the glory for my victory is Yours to keep forever.

In The Name of Jesus, Amen.

Day 5

God's Word For You Today:

IF GOD SAYS IT'S YOURS, TAKE IT

The Mandate

And David enquired at the LORD, saying, Shall I pursue after this troop? shall I overtake them? And he answered him, Pursue: for thou shalt surely overtake them, and without fail recover all (1 Samuel 30:8, KJV).

The Message

There is a very important lesson to be learned from this week's study passage, and it is this: when God says it's yours, take it! David does not delay. David does not hesitate. David is no longer discouraged. He rises, prepares for battle, and goes to seize what he has permission to take back by God. This is extremely important. Doubt defeats you before you ever get started. Dismay can derail you, but faith in God will always press you forward.

The Mission

Today, there are things in your life that God has given you permission to go and seize from the hand of satan. However, dismay, discouragement, disbelief, and even depression can sometimes cause you not to act when God says it's yours. Remember this: if God says it's yours, He is the owner of the deed of eminent domain, and it belongs to you.

The Meditation

Unto thee, O God, do I place my trust. Thankfully and joyfully, I have come into Your presence, and on this day, I celebrate Your sovereign reign over the enemy. Thank You for permitting me to go and to take back what's already mine.

In The Name of Jesus, Amen.

Day 6

God's Word For You Today:

GOOD NEWS: YOUR FIGHT IS FIXED

The Mandate

And David enquired at the LORD, saying, Shall I pursue after this troop? shall I overtake them? And he answered him, Pursue: for thou shalt surely overtake them, and without fail recover all (1 Samuel 30:8, KJV).

The Message

David does not worry about how he will win his fight. The idea of how he will win is never expressed in our passage, or anywhere else in the pericope. What is described is a fire-filled faithfulness that will move his fight forward. The good news of the passage is that David is acting as if his fight is already fixed! He is moving forward as if he has already won. As a believer in Jesus Christ, it is important for you to remember that your fight is fixed and you will win in the end. Your outcome has already been decided by the Lord, who sits in yesterday, rests in today, and awaits your arrival in tomorrow.

The Mission

If David can move forward like he has already won, why can't you? If David has an attitude that says, I win in the end over the enemy, why can't you? Today's message is a message of victory that comes to you by faith because your fight is already fixed. Live like it. Act like it. Pray like it. Praise like it and celebrate it. God has declared your victory, and there is no way for you to lose.

The Meditation

Today, O God, I thank You for victory in the name of Jesus, not because of how well I fight, but because You have fixed my fight before I ever got started. Today, I choose to move forward, and I choose to make sure everyone knows that God Himself gave me victory.

In The Name of Jesus, Amen.

Day 7

God's Word For You Today:

PERMISSION GRANTED, VICTORY GAINED

The Mandate

And David enquired at the LORD, saying, Shall I pursue after this troop? shall I overtake them? And he answered him, Pursue: for thou shalt surely overtake them, and without fail recover all (1 Samuel 30:8, KJV).

The Message

The most exciting part about today's passage is that David inquires, and God says yes. Whether the enemy is the factor or even David's faith is the answer, the bottom line is that David's God told him he could do what he was about to do, and David did it. The celebration in the passage is this: the outcome was already predetermined. Never forget this: if you walk with God, victory belongs to you. Your outcomes are predetermined. Your end has already been factored in from the very beginning.

The Mission

How do you usually act when victory finds your address? How do you typically celebrate when you know it's going to turn out for your good? How do you usually walk in faith when you know the answer is already pursuing you and victory is already yours? Today is a day where you live and fight like the outcome is predetermined, and you win in the end.

The Meditation

Today, O God, by faith, I thank You for victory over the enemy. I stand in complete solidarity with the truth of scripture, knowing that if You told me I could have it, if You told me I could possess it, if You told me it was mine, then it is mine from the moment You decreed it. And with your permission granted, I receive it.

In The Name of Jesus, Amen.

PERMISSION GRANTED Week 1

Now that you have completed week one, take a moment to sincerely reflect on your life, family, health, finances, faith, church, and community.

Now spend a quiet moment of prayerful solitude with God. Ask the Lord to show you what the enemy has his hands on that should be set free.

Ask the Lord for permission to take it back! Ask God to order your steps and show you what should be done.

Permission has been granted! What you must do now is walk by faith and not by sight. Obey the instructions, directions, and guidance of the Lord!

Day 1

God's Word For You Today:

HIS WAYS ARE NOT YOUR WAYS

The Mandate

So the people shouted when the priests blew with the trumpets: and it came to pass, when the people heard the sound of the trumpet, and the people shouted with a great shout, that the wall fell flat, so that the people went up into the city, every man straight before him, and they took the city (Joshua 6:20, KJV).

The Message

Our study passage for the week is filled with excitement. It's faithfully thrilling because God never does things our way. In short, His ways are not our ways. To capture a city, God doesn't appoint a new mayor. God doesn't shift the mindset of a city council member. What God does is so unique. He has His people march around the city, and on the seventh day and seventh lap around, He commands them to shout.

The Mission

If you are like most, when you look at your city, you can see the needs and things that must be done to make your city better and stronger. There are demonic strongholds that exist in many cities. There are satanic and luciferian spirits that sometimes guide and govern the politics of a town. But God is commissioning you to take your city back, and you do so by being obedient to His way, His will, and His Word.

The Meditation

So, God, I lift my city before You right now, and I ask in the name of Jesus Christ that You cause any spirit that is not like Yours to be dismissed. And we invite Your Spirit, the Holy Spirit, to reign supreme.

In The Name of Jesus, Amen.

Day 2

God's Word For You Today:

FOLLOWING FAVORED FEET

The Mandate

So the people shouted when the priests blew with the trumpets: and it came to pass, when the people heard the sound of the trumpet, and the people shouted with a great shout, that the wall fell flat, so that the people went up into the city, every man straight before him, and they took the city (Joshua 6:20, KJV).

The Message

If you are going to capture an entire city or municipality, you have to have a servant called by God who has favored feet. According to the story we're studying this week, Joshua has been handpicked by the Lord to lead Israel into the Promised Land. He is the one that the Lord has chosen. He is a vessel, a vehicle, and a vicar. As he leads the people, they are following a man who has favored feet. And as the people of God follow favored feet, their future is always brighter.

The Mission

As we study this week, you need to align yourself with the servant of the Lord who is going to follow the Lord's leadership no matter what. Individuals who are politically placed are placed by God, but they may or may not have favored feet. The servant called by God has favored feet, influence, impact, and spiritual power that God gives them to move things downtown, uptown, and around town.

The Meditation

God, bless my leader and my pastor with favored feet so that when my pastor shows up downtown, he is respected, highly honored, and one whom people will listen to and hear from God through.

In The Name of Jesus, Amen.

Day 3

God's Word For You Today:

HANDLE GOD'S BUSINESS AND HE WILL HANDLE YOURS

The Mandate
So the people shouted when the priests blew with the trumpets: and it came to pass, when the people heard the sound of the trumpet, and the people shouted with a great shout, that the wall fell flat, so that the people went up into the city, every man straight before him, and they took the city (Joshua 6:20, KJV).

The Message
The most exciting part of the narrative being studied this week is this: God lets His people know that when you handle His business, He handles your business. The Promised Land is currently occupied, but the people with the promise are following a man with favored feet as they march and prepare to take the city. It should be known that this is God's business. It is not the business of a 501(c)(3) nonprofit organization. It is not the business of a community organization. It is the business of the Kingdom of God to control the entire city.

The Mission
For a church to exist in a city without making an impact or influence on the town it sits in is a serious sin. It is the sin of lethargy. It is a sin that says, we don't care about what's going on around us. However, for a church to impact the city, influence a city, and call people in the city to be made better is a result of the manifestation of the Kingdom of God on earth. Your church should be a major influence in your city because you live in it and God lives in you.

The Meditation
O Lord, our Lord, how excellent is Your name in all the earth. My prayer today is that You would cause my church family to be a positive kingdom influence and impact on this entire municipality. Bless the city that I live in because it belongs to You.

In The Name of Jesus, Amen.

Day 4

God's Word For You Today:

DON'T JUST READ THE INSTRUCTIONS, OBEY THEM

The Mandate

So the people shouted when the priests blew with the trumpets: and it came to pass, when the people heard the sound of the trumpet, and the people shouted with a great shout, that the wall fell flat, so that the people went up into the city, every man straight before him, and they took the city (Joshua 6:20, KJV).

The Message

It's one thing to be given instructions; it's another thing to obey them. The blessing and benefit of obeying God is always the harvest and benefit of doing so. Joshua, in our passage this week, is obeying God to the letter. God tells Joshua, "march one time around the wall each day and say nothing," and Joshua does just that. He does it for six days. It should be duly noted that nothing changes on the days he marches until day seven, lap seven. There are times when you have to walk on with God, seeing no changes at all. And what God requires of you is for you to take another lap. Faith in God says, "I will obey You, and I will do it Your way."

The Mission

When you get prepared to take a city for the cause of Christ and the Kingdom of God on earth, be prepared to toil for a while without seeing any results. The results won't come until after you've labored long enough, toiled through tight and tempestuous times, and prayed fervently enough to watch God change things. Your faith will be rewarded because your obedience puts your faith into action.

The Meditation

God bless me with the faith of Job, the perseverance of David, the tenacity of Jeremiah, and the favor of Paul.

In The Name of Jesus, Amen.

Day 5

God's Word For You Today:

SOMETIMES NOISE IS COMPLETELY NECESSARY

The Mandate

So the people shouted when the priests blew with the trumpets: and it came to pass, when the people heard the sound of the trumpet, and the people shouted with a great shout, that the wall fell flat, so that the people went up into the city, every man straight before him, and they took the city (Joshua 6:20, KJV).

The Message

There are times when God does things that no one understands and commands things we do not comprehend. Such is the case in this week's study passage. Joshua is told to shout on a specific day at a particular time. More specifically, he is instructed to march seven times around the walls of Jericho and to shout on the seventh lap with the people and to have the horns blow. It's what I call an irony. This week, the idea is that sometimes noise is completely necessary. According to Hebrew history, silence is a sign of death and defeat. In this case, neither would be true. They are about to see victory like they've never seen it before, and they are vicars who are overcomers in the faith.

The Mission

There are times you should shout and declare victory with your mouth on purpose. When you are faced with a problem or a peril that's too big for you, but just right for God, give God victory in your praise and your worship that says, "God, this time, through You, I will overcome".

The Meditation

So, Lord, today I shout, thank You, Jesus, for the victory that came to me through the cross by Your word and through Your Spirit. I am not defeated. I am victorious.

In The Name of Jesus, Amen.

Day 6

God's Word For You Today:

IT WAS YOURS THE WHOLE TIME

The Mandate

So the people shouted when the priests blew with the trumpets: and it came to pass, when the people heard the sound of the trumpet, and the people shouted with a great shout, that the wall fell flat, so that the people went up into the city, every man straight before him, and they took the city (Joshua 6:20, KJV).

The Message

God sits in tomorrow while we live in today and holds yesterday in the hollow of His hand. This theory about God deals with God's omnipresence. It suggests that God is here, God is there, and God is everywhere. Once we comprehend this one truth about God, the truth of the passage comes into a whole new light. The victory was already Israel's the entire time. God was on both sides of the victory. He was the one leading them into battle, and He was also on the other side to help them triumph and realize that what He had already promised them was theirs from the beginning.

The Mission

Whatever it is you are praying for, fighting for, or asking God for, when you realize that God is already in the victory, already in the healing, already in your deliverance, you will see your problem and your conditions like He does. God sees your seasons of difficulty not as if you need a victory, but from the perspective that you already have won. He is on your side, and He cannot lose. The victory is yours from the beginning to the end. You win the entire time!

The Meditation

God, today, I thank You for victories I cannot see, the ability to overcome difficulties I have not yet faced, and forthcoming blessings that are earmarked for me. Thank You, Jesus, for being a God I can trust.

In The Name of Jesus, Amen.

Day 7
God's Word For You Today:
CAPTURE WHAT THE ENEMY THINKS IS CONQUERED

The Mandate
So the people shouted when the priests blew with the trumpets: and it came to pass, when the people heard the sound of the trumpet, and the people shouted with a great shout, that the wall fell down flat, so that the people went up into the city, every man straight before him, and they took the city (Joshua 6:20, KJV).

The Message
The story that has been studied this week is not just about marching and shouting. It is much more about believing, trusting, and obeying. It is about a city that the enemy thought was conquered, but God, through the favored feet of Joshua, captured it. The blessing of this week's study is to remind us as believers in Jesus Christ that what God says is yours is yours, even if it's an entire city. If the Lord declares the municipality belongs to you, then live like it, act like it, walk like it, and talk like it.

The Mission
At this time in this study, by now, you should see what God decrees and declares will always come to pass. There is never a time a declaration comes from God as a promise that goes unfulfilled. It may be delayed, but it will never be denied.

The Meditation
Today, O Lord, I lift my city, where I live, to You. There are corners of the city that have been captured by demonic influence, violence, evil, and sometimes satanic setbacks. But today, I declare victory for my city in faith, knowing what the devil thinks he has captured will never be conquered by him, because You own it.

In The Name of Jesus, Amen.

PERMISSION GRANTED Week 2

A city is a reflection of its citizens. As a citizen of your municipality, you should impact it in ways that leave an indelible imprint on it for the cause of Christ and the sake of the Kingdom of God on earth. With this in mind, you have permission to take your whole city back! Here are some great ideas on "how to" do just that.

Partner with your Church in Community Related Affairs
Get actively involved with other Community-Based Organizations
Get to know your Elected City Officials
Attend a City Council Meeting
Develop a Neighborhood Association
Organize a Street Watch Program
Participate in Municipal Activities
Organize a Neighborhood Clean-Up Day
Develop a Prayer Walk Through Your Community
Implement Activities for Children as Safe Summer Opportunities

If anyone asks you what you are doing, tell them you are taking your city back one positive event at a time. Start small, organize well, be consistent, and what you develop will grow in grace to impact your city in amazing ways.

Day 1

God's Word For You Today:

TRUST ME, IT'S ONLY A TEST

The Mandate
And the LORD turned the captivity of Job, when he prayed for his friends: also the LORD gave Job twice as much as he had before (Job 42:10, KJV).

The Message
The book of Job is a dynamic narrative that exposes the truth about God as it relates to testing those who love Him. Believers who love God will all be tested at some point in their pilgrimage on the planet. Testing and blessing are always interconnected. With great blessing sometimes comes huge testing. Job's test is severe: the loss of money, the loss of family, the loss of children, and the loss of his health at one point. God even allows satan to cross-examine the witness while he's on the witness stand. But Job understands one key component: it's a test, and by faith in the Lord, He will overcome.

The Mission
There are times in your life, as you walk with Jesus Christ, that you, too, will be tested. In fact, at this very moment, as you read this devotional lesson, there may be some tests you are enduring. Keep this in mind: the way to survive a test is to be faithful to God until the test is over.

The Meditation
Lord, I do realize faith not tested should not be trusted. Help me, O God. Please give me the strength to endure.

In The Name of Jesus, Amen.

Day 2

God's Word For You Today:

PRESSURE CHANGES EVERYTHING

The Mandate

And the LORD turned the captivity of Job, when he prayed for his friends: also the LORD gave Job twice as much as he had before (Job 42:10, KJV).

The Message

God knows exactly how much pressure Job can handle. While satan may be allowed to test Job, God is the One fostering the entire examination. It's a lot of pressure, but pressure changes everything, just not everything for the positive. In some instances, pressure crushes things. However, in some different examinations, pressure makes things stronger and better. In the life of Job and the life of every believer, there are times when pressure makes us more precious in the sight of the Lord.

The Mission

There are times in your life when you have to endure moments of severe pressure. The blessing of the Lord is knowing that the same God who allowed it would be your strength to help you survive it. It's like having a cheat sheet for an examination that the teacher gives. It's hard to fail when you already have the answers in your hand.

The Meditation

Lord, I pray right now for a spirit of an overcomer, of one who endures. With You, I realize I cannot fail, and with You, I celebrate the fact that I have already overcome.

In The Name of Jesus, Amen.

Day 3

God's Word For You Today:

PEOPLE CAN HURT YOU AND NOT EVEN KNOW IT

The Mandate

And the LORD turned the captivity of Job, when he prayed for his friends: also the LORD gave Job twice as much as he had before (Job 42:10, KJV).

The Message

Job is surrounded by three (supposed) friends during his time of immense testing and suffering. Their names are Eliphaz, Bildad, and Zophar: a negativist, a pacifist, and an extremist. They mean well, but their outcomes are often more harmful than helpful. They look at Job from different perspectives, and they're not trying to hurt him, but their presence, comments, and expressed thoughts do more harm than good.

The Mission

Have you ever had people who really meant you well harm you? Have you ever had friends who wanted to offer you sound advice but had nothing meaningful to say? Have you ever been surrounded by people whose comments crushed you instead of building or edifying you? Such is the case with Job. Keep this in mind: the most excellent counselor you will ever have is the counsel that comes from Christ Himself.

The Meditation

Bless the Lord, O my soul, and all that's within me. I bless Your holy name. I thank You, O God, for the people who have hurt me, because when they have hurt me the most, You have shown Yourself the most significant help I would ever need. Today, I thank You for being my only true help.

In The Name of Jesus, Amen.

Day 4

God's Word For You Today:

SHIFT THE CONVERSATION AND PRAY SOMETHING

The Mandate

And the LORD turned the captivity of Job, when he prayed for his friends: also the LORD gave Job twice as much as he had before (Job 42:10, KJV).

The Message

As Job sits in the unwise counsel of his alleged friends, he suddenly decides to shift the conversation and starts to pray for them. In short, Job stops talking to them about his condition and begins to speak to God. This gives us a powerful, poignant, pointed picture of the power of prayer itself. If we learn nothing from the story of Job in the Bible, remember these two key facets: God allows tests, and prayer still works. The prayer of Job changes the trajectory of his entire outcome.

The Mission

God awaits us to pray to Him, especially during times of testing and trial. Job prays to the Lord in Job 42:10, and it changes everything. The conversation shifts from his supposed friends talking to Job to Job praying to God. This change shifts everything for the better and for the best in the life of the man who needs God the most. The same principle applies to every Christian. Talking about your problems to others only celebrates the problem. However, when you speak to the Problem Solver about your problems, you take back what the enemy thought he could keep.

The Meditation

O God, it is at this very moment that I have decided to shift my conversation. I want You to know I am leaning, depending, and relying on You for healing and restoration that can only come from Your hand to my heart. Thank You, Lord Jesus, for hearing my prayers and petitions.

In The Name of Jesus, Amen.

Day 5

God's Word For You Today:

SHOOV MEANS IT'S TURNING IN YOUR FAVOR

The Mandate

And the LORD turned the captivity of Job, when he prayed for his friends: also the LORD gave Job twice as much as he had before (Job 42:10, KJV).

The Message

Notice the scripture reads, "And the Lord turned the captivity of Job when he prayed for his friends." The word used, "turned" in the Hebrew, is *shoov*, and shoov means it's turning in your favor. It means to flip the script on something. It suggests moving from a negative to a positive, from nothing to something, from bad to good, from darkness to light, from weakness to strength, from defeat to victory, and from being overcome to becoming an overcomer. Job encounters the shift that says it's turning around for me.

The Mission

At this very moment, you can trust God with flipping the script on your current reality that needs His favor the most. God specializes in turning things around and working in your favor. The favor of the Lord is real, and His ability to control an outcome is never parallel to anything on earth. His power is unmatched, and He can do what He says He can do. When God decides to flip the script on your season of suffering, do not forget to add what He did for you to your already existing testimony that says, "the devil had it, but I got it all back!"

The Meditation

Lord Jesus, thank You for turning it around in my favor. I understand that what you have for me is mine. That includes healing, restoration, deliverance, and blessing in the only name that matters the most.

In The Name of Jesus, Amen.

Day 6

God's Word For You Today:

YOUR INCREASE IS A PART OF GOD'S PLAN

The Mandate

And the LORD turned the captivity of Job, when he prayed for his friends: also the LORD gave Job twice as much as he had before (Job 42:10, KJV).

The Message

One of the greatest blessings of reading the entire Book of Job is knowing that it doesn't end the way it began. It began with a wealthy man, blessed with everything he could imagine: a loving family, faith, good physical health, a steady supply of food, a comfortable home, and a fulfilling job. Yet the Bible gives us the truth about his suffering and his losses. The shout and the celebration of this story, however, is this: God gave him more in the conclusion of the narrative than he had at the outset. In short, his increase was a part of God's plan the entire time.

The Mission

It may seem like you're going through a season of losses, but when God grants permission for you to overcome and endure, you get more in the conclusion than you did at the very beginning. Your story will end with you being blessed and favored by the Lord. The idea is that your testing is the root of the blessing that will produce the favor of the Lord in your life like never before.

The Meditation

Spirit of the Living God, fall afresh on me. Let Your blessing rest on me. Let Your favor rest within me. Thank You for the increase that is headed my direction even now.

In The Name of Jesus, Amen.

Day 7

God's Word For You Today:

DOUBLE FOR YOUR TROUBLE

The Mandate
And the LORD turned the captivity of Job, when he prayed for his friends: also the LORD gave Job twice as much as he had before (Job 42:10, KJV).

The Message
Reread the verse that's been studied for the week. Look at it carefully. As you study it, pay close attention to the last clause, or what's called the final clause of the verse. It reads like this, "and the Lord gave Job twice as much as he had before." The phrase "twice as much" implies that Job receives double compensation for his trouble. In other words, if Job has no trouble or no time of testing, he does not get double. But because he's endured, persevered, and overcame, he not only gets back what he lost, but he gains double for his trouble. Here is the idea that's presented in the text, and its truth will last forever: if you want double, you must endure the trouble. However, if you endure the trouble, God has a holy habit of giving you double for everything the enemy took from you.

The Mission
There are times you go through seasons of losses, and God permits you to take back what you've lost. It comes through prayer, it comes through patience, and it comes through perseverance. If you can endure, just as God blessed Job through the channel of testing, He will do the same for you.

The Meditation
Spirit of the Living God, rest, rule, and remain with me so that I can endure my season of testing and come out with increase and overflow that I have to give You the glory.

In The Name of Jesus, Amen.

PERMISSION GRANTED Week 3

The Lord of heaven wants your life free and faithfully in His hands every day, all day long. For this liberty to happen, you must look at areas of your life where there may be issues of spiritual bondage. In our Bible lesson this week, Job's struggle was with supposed friends whom he needed to forgive. When he forgave them and prayed for them, the Lord restored what had been taken by his enemies, and he received double for his trouble.

With this in mind, in what areas of your life do you have areas of personal struggle? Take a moment today and sincerely seek the Lord about it, and turn it over to Him.

The great news of the day is this: permission has been granted, and the liberty given by the Lord should be your expectation.

Day 1

God's Word For You Today:

YOU'VE GOT SOME IN YOUR FAMILY TOO

The Mandate

And the LORD looked upon him, and said, Go in this thy might, and thou shalt save Israel from the hand of the Midianites: have not I sent thee (Judges 6:14, KJV).

The Message

This week, we are studying an exciting passage found in Judges Chapter 6. It's the story of Gideon, Israel, their disobedience, and rebellion. Their prayer to God and His answer of deliverance and liberty. It's important to understand that this story has at its core people who are near you who rebel against God, which causes God to become angry with us. Here's the truth: we have some in every family. My family has some. Your family has some. Our families have people in them who disobey God.

The Mission

When you come to grips with the fact that no one is perfect, and all of us need God, it will cause us to get to the foot of the throne of God and ask God to help us, to have mercy upon us, to repent, to recover, to recoup, and to restore us to where we belong in Him.

The Meditation

Eternal God, our Father, look now on my family. Father, if we have sinned against You in any way, forgive us. But Lord, for those who are still bound that bear my last name, forgive us, heal us, strengthen us, and bring us to liberty in You that gives us freedom in the faith.

In The Name of Jesus, Amen.

Day 2

God's Word For You Today:

DISOBEDIENCE CAUSED IT, BUT GRACE IS ABOUT TO CHANGE IT

The Mandate

And the LORD looked upon him, and said, Go in this thy might, and thou shalt save Israel from the hand of the Midianites: have not I sent thee (Judges 6:14, KJV).

The Message

When you read Judges Chapter 6, beginning with verse 1, you'll discover that Israel's disobedience caused the entire collapse of their country, of their families. Here in the text, Israel has done what God told them not to do. The record reads like this: "And Israel did evil in the sight of the Lord." The Bible is not emphatically clear on precisely what evil they did, but here is what we do know: disobedience caused the wrath of God to find them. The great news about today's lesson is this: disobedience caused it, but God's grace is about to change it.

The Mission

The Lord Jesus Christ is a God who answers prayers. He is a gracious, loving, caring, and compassionate Lord. Just as He showed Israel grace time and time again, our God does the same for us. There are times when the evil that enslaves the Christian comes because of disobedience and not ignorance, as many suggest. The blessing is found in the truth of God's grace that meets you right where you are. This is done for two reasons: to let the enemy know that you belong to God and to remind you that God has not given up on you.

The Meditation

O Lord, our Lord, how excellent is Thy name in all the earth. This day, O God, I have come to ask You for Your grace for the sins and the errors of my ways. Thank You for giving me another chance.

In The Name of Jesus, Amen.

Day 3

God's Word For You Today:

GET TO THE RIGHT LOCATION

The Mandate

And the LORD looked upon him, and said, Go in this thy might, and thou shalt save Israel from the hand of the Midianites: have not I sent thee (Judges 6:14, KJV).

The Message

In our study passage this week, Gideon has been called by God to deliver Israel from the hands of the Midianites. The Midianites are the enemies of Israel, who have been allowed and permitted by God to oppress the Israelites as discipline because of Israel's disobedience. The turning point in today's Bible narrative is found when God takes a moment to summon one of us to help the rest of us. Gideon's task is to reach the correct location to perform the work that God is calling him to do. In short, not any location will do. He must be where the Lord has called him.

The Mission

There are times when you are where you are by tradition, and other times you are where you are by habit. However, there comes a moment where God has work for you to do, and it requires that you be put, placed, and planted in the place that God has ordained for you. The question today is, where has God ordained you to be? You will never, ever get all that you want out of life and never see deliverance that comes from His throne until you are in the correct location.

The Meditation

God, order my steps, guide my thoughts, plant my feet, sow my life into the soul of divine purpose so that what comes from it is liberation and blessing for me and those connected to me.

In The Name of Jesus, Amen.

Day 4

God's Word For You Today:

YOU CAN'T TAKE EVERYBODY WITH YOU

The Mandate

And the LORD looked upon him, and said, Go in this thy might, and thou shalt save Israel from the hand of the Midianites: have not I sent thee (Judges 6:14, KJV).

The Message

One of the most exciting segments of the story of Gideon versus the Midianites is this: God allows Gideon to take a massive army of about 30,000 men to battle. However, as Gideon gets closer to the Midianite camp, God decides to decrease the number of soldiers he's traveling with who are prepared to do combat. When you look carefully at the entire narrative, God reduces an army of 30,000 men to 300 men. Those that the Lord chooses are not really the best soldiers to fight with. In short, what the Lord was telling Gideon was, "with me on your side, you don't need everybody else with you. I am more than enough."

The Mission

There are times when we really think we can take everybody with us. We have in our mindset a philosophy that says, the more the merrier. We believe that we are a majority if we have more people with us. But here is the truth: anything is a majority with God attached. As long as you have Him, you have it all.

The Meditation

God, as I prayerfully fight for my family, please make me a majority when it comes to fighting for my sons, my daughters, my kinsmen, and those who are connected to me. In my heart, O Lord, they are worth fighting for and saving.

In The Name of Jesus, Amen.

Day 5

God's Word For You Today:

BE PREPARED TO DO STUFF THAT MAKES NO SENSE

The Mandate

And the LORD looked upon him, and said, Go in this thy might, and thou shalt save Israel from the hand of the Midianites: have not I sent thee (Judges 6:14, KJV).

The Message

This is where the plot thickens, and this is where the narrative makes absolutely no sense. Gideon's army has been reduced from 30,000 soldiers to 300 soldiers. And to make matters worse, he's about to fight the Midianites. When Gideon approaches the battlefield, God gives him instructions that make no sense at all. Gideon is told to break jars, crash glasses, scream, and shout. And, from this noise-making, which seems like nonsense, the Lord would somehow cause him to come out victorious. The great news of the day is that Gideon is obedient enough to do it, and victory finds him. His enemies are defeated.

The Mission

If faith makes sense to you, it's no longer faith. It's a scientific fact that you can put your arms around and figure it out. The truth of the matter is, faith that's genuine faith, makes absolutely no sense. It's why it takes faith to believe it, and even more faith to act upon it. The journey that you will take to gain back what the enemy has taken in your family will be a matter of faith. Faith for the fight, the future, and your family.

The Meditation

God, where I doubt, give me belief; where I struggle, give me strength; and where my faith is feeble, make my faith strong for the fight, because my family is worth it.

In The Name of Jesus, Amen.

Day 6

God's Word For You Today:

IF YOU'VE GOT THE FAITH, GOD'S GOT THE POWER

The Mandate

And the LORD looked upon him, and said, Go in this thy might, and thou shalt save Israel from the hand of the Midianites: have not I sent thee (Judges 6:14, KJV).

The Message

If you remember nothing else about today's devotional lesson, remember this: if you've got the faith, God's got the power. Faith is acting like a thing is so, even when it's not so, so that it might be so! Faith is trusting God in the dark, not walking blindly, but walking believing in God. Faith is trusting God when nothing else seems to make sense. Faith is the substance of things hoped for and the evidence of things not seen. Faith works when nothing else does. If we learn nothing else about Gideon, Israel, faith, and family, it should be this: if you want God to save your family, it will have to be done by faith.

The Mission

There will come a moment when you fight for your family. When the moment of spiritual battle finds your address, remember this: when it seems like it's falling apart and there are only a few still left, your faith in God matters the most. Faith matters when it seems like prayers are not answered, and faith really matters when it seems like all hope is futile. If your faith is strong, you will see the promises of God come to pass and the adversary of the cross suffer defeat. By faith, your family will win!

The Meditation

Eternal God, our Father, lay Your hands on my family. And wherever there is anything that displeases you, remove it. And if there are any that are unsaved in our ranks, deliver, rescue, and save them.

In The Name of Jesus, Amen.

Day 7

God's Word For You Today:

IT'S WORTH THE FIGHT

The Mandate

And the LORD looked upon him, and said, Go in this thy might, and thou shalt save Israel from the hand of the Midianites: have not I sent thee (Judges 6:14, KJV).

The Message

Some fights are not worth it. Fighting over simple disputes that could have been easily resolved has led to more catastrophes than we could ever come to grips with. Fights over money. Fights over policy. It seems like everyone is fighting these days. Even in this week's study passage, there's a fight between Israel, Gideon, and Midian. Yet some fights are worth it. When it comes to fighting for your mind, your health, your wealth, your family, those who you love and hold dear, it's worth the fight. If you don't fight, it suggests that what you're fighting for is futile.

The Mission

Look at your family carefully. Consider your loved ones deeply and all those who are still alive who share your kinship, friendship, and close relationships. Today's lesson and this week's study passage have been designed for you to know that when it comes to your family, their salvation, blessing, and their freedom, your faith in God is worth the fight.

The Meditation

Eternal God, our Father, today I thank You for those who are related to me, friendship, kinship, and the like. I pray for each one of them, for their walk to be with You, for their witness to be for You, and for the warfare that we use for our families to come to full fruition because of You.

In The Name of Jesus, Amen.

<u>PERMISSION GRANTED Week 4</u>

Perhaps your family is like most; if so, it needs prayer. In each family, there are people who are victims of generational curses, systemic family illnesses, and poverty that seems to never come to an end. In some families, relational issues such as jealousy, envy, pride, hatred, and unforgiveness may also arise.

Take a close look at your family. Realize that if your family is going to experience the favor of the Lord, someone will have to fight for God to move mightily within its ranks. With this in mind, make a prayer list consisting of the members of your family and the things that you know they need from God. Make a secret place in your home where you meet God for prayer for the next eleven weeks.

Pray for your family like never before! And, remember this, PERMISSION HAS BEEN GRANTED for you to prayerfully fight for them, knowing that victory is already yours through the blood of the cross.

Your family is worth fighting for, so fight for them in prayer!

Day 1

God's Word For You Today:

I FEEL LIKE SOMEBODY IS ROBBING ME

The Mandate

25 And I will restore to you the years that the locust hath eaten, the cankerworm, and the caterpillar, and the palmerworm, my great army which I sent among you. 26 And ye shall eat in plenty, and be satisfied, and praise the name of the LORD your God, that hath dealt wondrously with you: and my people shall never be ashamed.

The Message

Our study passage for the week will be the book of Joel, chapter 2. The chapter can be divided into three segments. In the first section of chapter 2, God pours out His wrath. The second section of the chapter shifts to a merciful God who permits and allows time for repentance. The latter part of the chapter deals with restoration. In a contemporary light, the closing segment of chapter 2 deals with cash, crops, and comebacks. It deals emphatically with the financial prosperity of God's people despite their disobedience. God makes room for their restoration. In short, God gives Israel back what the enemy thinks he can keep.

The Mission

No matter how bad your finances may be at this very moment, God is a God who can and will restore you. God uses moments, times, seasons, and even utter poverty to reveal Himself to His people. The great news attached to the power of God rests within His ability to alter outcomes. God alone can turn things around and make them work in your favor. With the Lord on your side, you can go from poverty to plenty, from nothing to something, and from just enough to more than enough. The God you serve is an amazing God.

The Meditation

O Lord, my God, bless the resources You have placed in my hand that actually belong to You. Favor my finances so that I never feel like anyone is robbing me ever again.

In The Name of Jesus, Amen.

Day 2

God's Word For You Today:

NO CROPS, NO CASH

The Mandate

25 *And I will restore to you the years that the locust hath eaten, the cankerworm, and the caterpillar, and the palmerworm, my great army which I sent among you.* 26 *And ye shall eat in plenty, and be satisfied, and praise the name of the* LORD *your God, that hath dealt wondrously with you: and my people shall never be ashamed.*

The Message

Joel 2:25-26 brings an excitement to the reader as we look and consider the fact that God is about to restore what the cankerworm, caterpillar, and palmerworm destroyed. A great army was sent to destroy Israel and is now about to be set aside, and restoration is going to be at its best. In fact, there is a sharp difference between what is presented in verse 25 and what is promised in verse 26. In verse 25, God says restoration is coming, and in verse 26, Israel will "eat the plenty" of the land. The difference here is simple: no crops, no cash. With crops, you have cash. What this text speaks to is the restoration of their fiduciary measure.

The Mission

If God can restore Israel's prosperity, He has the same power to do even more for you. With this in mind, the Lord is the same yesterday, today, and forever. The great news about restoration from God is that it is never unidimensional. It is always multi-dimensional. When the Lord of heaven restores you, it is akin to raindrops falling from the sky. The rain falls everywhere. Some drops fall on your health, while some fall on your family, your faith, and even your finances. Restoration in your finances affects every part of your life.

The Meditation

Eternal God our Father, restore my financial prospectus today. Take what I have, include Yourself in it, and bless Yourself through it.

In The Name of Jesus, Amen.

Day 3

God's Word For You Today:

IF HE'S DONE IT BEFORE, HE CAN DO IT AGAIN

The Mandate
25 And I will restore to you the years that the locust hath eaten, the cankerworm, and the caterpillar, and the palmerworm, my great army which I sent among you. 26 And ye shall eat in plenty, and be satisfied, and praise the name of the LORD your God, that hath dealt wondrously with you: and my people shall never be ashamed.

The Message
The grace of God and His strength before humankind are never an isolated incident. In other words, what God has done before, He can do again. This idea of financial restoration is not mentioned for the first time here in Joel. God has always been one who restores His people. Of course, there are moments God permits and allows enemy attacks, tough times, and even demonic influences to test His people. However, the best news of the day is found in Joel 2:25-26: God is going to restore His people again, and nothing can stop it.

The Mission
The benefit of knowing God is this: He never leaves you in the same state that He found you. Even in times of disobedience, lack of repentance, and in some instances, rebellion, God proves to be gracious. Receive this news and hold it close to your heart. The Lord is a God of grace, mercy, and another chance.

The Meditation
God, my finances need another chance. There have been times, Lord, that I have used the resources You have given me without thought of solid faithful stewardship. Forgive me and restore what is in my hand so that I can flourish, have plenty, and see the satisfaction of my family in the faith.

In The Name of Jesus, Amen.

Day 4

God's Word For You Today:

WATCH HOW YOU HANDLE HIM

The Mandate

25 *And I will restore to you the years that the locust hath eaten, the cankerworm, and the caterpillar, and the palmerworm, my great army which I sent among you.* 26 *And ye shall eat in plenty, and be satisfied, and praise the name of the LORD your God, that hath dealt wondrously with you: and my people shall never be ashamed.*

The Message

Be careful how you handle God. There are moments in Israel's walk where they treat God as if He were some good luck charm, exploiting His goodness, to gain from Him, but then fail to obey and worship Him sincerely. There have been moments in Israel's life history where the grace of God has been wasted and the mercy of God has been taken for granted. The warning we gain from the restoration of Joel 2 is simply this: watch how you handle Him. Handle Him like your future depends on it. Handle Him like your life depends on it. Handle Him like your financial future is in His hands, because it is.

The Mission

There comes a moment when introspective theological thought should be given to how we really treat God. To honor, obey, and follow Him in faith is our benefit and blessing regarding how we handle the treasure that is rightfully His. In the Christian faith, there is a difference between stewardship and ownership. We are the stewards. God is the owner.

The Meditation

Lord, teach me to use what You have given me so that what You have given me brings You glory.

In The Name of Jesus, Amen.

Day 5

God's Word For You Today:

RESTORATION IS HEADED YOUR WAY

The Mandate

25 And I will restore to you the years that the locust hath eaten, the cankerworm, and the caterpillar, and the palmerworm, my great army which I sent among you. 26 And ye shall eat in plenty, and be satisfied, and praise the name of the LORD your God, that hath dealt wondrously with you: and my people shall never be ashamed.

The Message

The blessing of this segment of the passage brings to the forefront a God who is about to restore His people from the hand of the adversary. Take a moment and reread just verse 25, and as you reread it, pay close attention to the "I will" that opens the verse and the promise of restoration for the years the locust had destroyed the crops. Keep in mind that the locust is a symbol of destruction here, and the crops represent their financial prosperity. God is about to restore them. The blessing of the day after reading Joel 2:25-26 is the promise from the Lord that grants restoration to His people, even though they do not deserve it and have not earned it.

The Mission

There are times when grace and gratitude should meet, and they should become friends at the very least. When God promises restoration in the midst of what appears to be economic decline, it deserves a moment of gratitude, because the Lord's grace continues to make a way for those who believe. The miracle of the text is that nowhere in it does Israel plow or pluck. They don't have to worry about seed time and harvest, because there is a former and a latter rain that God will provide. It is God's grace and blessing causing the restoration to come to pass.

The Meditation

Thank You, O Lord, for restoring what You've placed in my hand. I bless Your name for increase, and I give You the glory for overflow.

In The Name of Jesus, Amen.

Day 6

God's Word For You Today:

DON'T FORGET WHERE IT ALL CAME FROM

The Mandate

25 *And I will restore to you the years that the locust hath eaten, the cankerworm, and the caterpillar, and the palmerworm, my great army which I sent among you.* 26 *And ye shall eat in plenty, and be satisfied, and praise the name of the LORD your God, that hath dealt wondrously with you: and my people shall never be ashamed.*

The Message

There comes a moment when you must give God glory for everything you have, because without Him, you have nothing, and with Him, you have it all. There is an important message in this week's verse, and it is this: when the Lord blesses you, and He shall, when God restores the things that were once economically challenged, and He will, do not forget where it all came from. Every blessing has come from God's throne to your hand, from His goodness to your lack, from Him directly to you. Never, ever forget that.

The Mission

The glory of the Lord is made manifest when His people are restored during conditions that seem unlikely. It doesn't matter what the conditions look like. It only matters that God blesses us, despite the conditions that surround us, and that He favors us so that His blessing is our gift.

The Meditation

O Lord, our Lord, how excellent is Thy name in all the earth. When we pause to consider just how wonderful You've been, we realize we are debtors to Your grace. We are overwhelmed with thanksgiving for Your mercy, and we celebrate Your love. Thank You for divine provision, meeting our needs, and even providing an overflow.

In The Name of Jesus, Amen.

Day 7

God's Word For You Today:

A MONETARY COMEBACK IS WHAT YOU ARE LOOKING FOR

The Mandate

25 And I will restore to you the years that the locust hath eaten, the cankerworm, and the caterpillar, and the palmerworm, my great army which I sent among you. 26 And ye shall eat in plenty, and be satisfied, and praise the name of the LORD your God, that hath dealt wondrously with you: and my people shall never be ashamed.

The Message

Restoration, in our study passage for the week, comes from a Hebrew word that means to put a bone back in place. Israel had been through some tough times filled with locusts and cankerworms, the caterpillar and the palmerworm. These insects had been like a fracture of a bone in the leg of a soldier who could no longer run or fight. The good news is that God restored everything they destroyed. Here is the best news of the passage: the monetary comeback that was needed has been provided. God had once again granted the substance Israel needed from their crops to produce the cash that would bless them and enable them to survive.

The Mission

If you are looking for a monetary comeback and you are a faithful steward of what you possess, remember this: God will provide it, so start saying thank you for what's headed your direction right now. Thank You is always appropriate for the God who says, "I'm not going to leave your finances in the same state they were in one year ago." The blessing of watching the Lord work things out for His people is discovered when He provides a shift that cannot be explained, but is evident all the same. Give God glory for the shift that is coming to pass in your life regarding your finances. The Lord has the final say so regarding your spiritual peace and your financial portion.

The Meditation

Lord, to say thank You for the increase You're getting ready to provide for me is not enough. I vow and promise as I am blessed with what You put in my hand. I will increase Your kingdom on earth so that what is in Your hand may continue to be spread around the world for the sake of the Gospel.

In The Name of Jesus, Amen.

PERMISSION GRANTED Week 5

Hear these words for the final time this week, "And ye shall eat in plenty......" These words do not guarantee wealth, but they do promise provision. With this in mind, take a moment to examine your financial situation carefully. Develop a plan of fiduciary faithfulness, which should include tithing and giving as a Disciple of Jesus Christ.

Give ten percent of your net pay to the Lord as a tithe. Secondly, save ten percent and place it in your savings account. Take the remaining eighty percent and use it for fixed and variable costs you incur each pay cycle. For example, your net pay (compensation after tax deductions) is $1,000.00. Here is what you should do. Give the Lord's church $100.00. After you give the tithe, then pay your savings account $100.00. Live within the financial confines of $800.00.

The windows of heaven are about to open in your direction, and the favor of the Lord will without fail find your finances. Increase will be your testimony, and God's faithfulness will be your blessing.

Remember this simple financial faith formula and practice it each time you have Kingdom resources in your hands: 10% (tithe), 10% (save), and 80% (live on this amount of money).

Day 1

God's Word For You Today:

HE'S A THIEF

The Mandate

Neither give place to the devil (Eph. 4:27, KJV).

The Message

The Apostle Paul penned this masterpiece of a letter, which we will spend the week reading. Our focus for the week will be Ephesians 4. In this chapter, Paul makes it very clear that we have one Lord, one faith, and one baptism. One God who is above all and in all. The great Apostle presses his argument by teaching key Christian principles. For instance, there are some things that we need to take off and other things we should put on. There are things we should tolerate and other things we should no longer accept. In the element of his teaching us not to accept things, Paul says, "neither give place to the devil." It was his way of saying, I want all of my possessions back because the devil is not just a liar, he's a thief.

The Mission

Hear this wisdom and apply it to your life: do not believe the lies of the devil. A liar lies because lying is what they do. Know this: the devil is a liar. Here is more wisdom that is life-changing once applied to your life by faith: when you know a thief is a thief, you should always treat them like one. Jesus has labeled the enemy who stands against us as a thief who comes to steal, kill, and destroy. Do not be shocked when the enemy makes a gallant effort to lie and steal from you and yours. Expect it. Anticipate it. Prepare your life for it!

The Meditation

Today, O God, I have decided not to let the devil have anything You died for me to possess. If You died for me to have it, I plan to hold on to it, keep it, and give You glory for it.

In The Name of Jesus, Amen.

Day 2

God's Word For You Today:

WHAT DOES HE HAVE THAT HE TOOK FROM YOU

The Mandate
Neither give place to the devil (Eph. 4:27, KJV).

The Message
When Paul teaches the Ephesian church not to let the devil have a place, what he was essentially saying is keep the enemy out of your face and away from your space. Here is why: if you allow him in your space and in your face, you will have a list of things he's stolen from you that you don't even realize he possesses. Take a moment, survey the landscape of your human existence, and ask yourself this question: what did the enemy take from me?

The Mission
If you are wise and faithful, you would make up your mind right now regarding things the enemy has taken from you. Just because the enemy has it does not mean you're going to let him keep it. You are going to take back what he has stolen from you. The thief steals, yet your God gives. The blessing of Ephesians 4 is that God gave some prophets, some apostles, some evangelists, some pastors, and teachers for the perfecting of the saints, for the work of the ministry. Let this ministry, which He has given us, work on your behalf.

The Meditation
Today, Lord, I do not come to lay claim on anything but to repossess what has already been promised and to faithfully claim what is already mine. Thank You, Jesus, for being a God of restoration, and I thank You for Your favor that rests upon my life.

In The Name of Jesus, Amen.

Day 3

God's Word For You Today:

IF YOU GIVE HIM AN INCH, HE'LL BECOME YOUR RULER

The Mandate
Neither give place to the devil (Eph. 4:27, KJV).

The Message
One of the reasons why Paul cautions the church at Ephesus not to give place to the devil is due to the enemy's aggressive behavior. If you give him an inch, he'll want to become your ruler. The enemy is very sneaky, sly, slick, and even in many cases, deadly. If you let him in, he doesn't want to take the ride. He wants to drive. He wants to control what you have and what he can take from you, that the blood of the lamb has purchased as a ransom for you to possess.

The Mission
Do not let the devil have anything God has given you. To let him have it as a thief suggests Jesus didn't pay enough for it when He died. The truth of the matter is, our God paid with the blood of His own Son so that what the Son has provided, His children, like you, can take advantage of.

The Meditation
Great is the Lord, and greatly is He to be praised. O magnify the Lord with me and let us exalt His name together. Lord, I've come to say thank You because You are the only ruler that I will ever have in my life. No matter what the devil desires, his inch shall never equate to him being my ruler. You're my ruler, and every inch of my soul belongs to You.

In The Name of Jesus, Amen.

Day 4

God's Word For You Today:

RESIST HIM AND REJECT HIM

The Mandate

Neither give place to the devil (Eph. 4:27, KJV).

The Message

There is a slight misconception regarding how believers engage the enemy. True enough, we engage the enemy in spiritual warfare. However, an idea is circulating that is a misinterpretation of what God has given us in the faith as Christians. Some think we can bind the devil, as if we have the power of constraint over him. This is erroneous. We have the power to resist the devil. However, we do not bind him because binding him requires a throne. As Christians, we are not enthroned; we are empowered. Only God has a throne. Therefore, we are empowered to resist the devil (James 4:7, KJV). In short, God has graciously granted us the right to look the enemy in the face and tell the devil, "hell no!"

The Mission

There comes a time when we must resist the devil and reject the enemy. This authority comes from God, and the ability to do it comes from God's hand to your heart by faith. To stand flat-footed and reject what the enemy has to offer is our bona fide benefit. Use this authority to be wise and practice it to be holy.

The Meditation

O God of Heaven, thank You for the strength to resist and reject the enemy. I give You glory for the decisions You have influenced in my life to tell the devil no.

In The Name of Jesus, Amen.

Day 5

God's Word For You Today:

TO SAY NO TO THE ENEMY IS TO SAY YES TO THE ADVOCATE

The Mandate
Neither give place to the devil (Eph. 4:27, KJV).

The Message
When Paul empowers the Ephesian church with the verse we have been studying this week, the idea behind it is not just to say no to the devil, but to say yes to the Lord our God. To say no to the adversary is to say yes to the advocate. What empowers us as Christians most is not the answer of 'no,' where we yield to the enemy; it's the 'yes,' where we submit our lives to the will of our advocate. To tell God yes is to say, "Lord, I will live life Your way, and I will not let the devil have anything that belongs to You that comes to me."

The Mission
There comes a moment in your walk with God where you must resist the enemy, and to resist him effectively, you must say yes to God. Your 'yes' to God will guide other decisions for you once you've made up your mind. To say yes to God answers all other questions for you, and it also rejects all other ideas that are not in compliance with the promises of the Prince of Peace. When you tell God 'yes' and mean it, telling the devil 'no' will be much easier for you to do.

The Meditation
Lord, I celebrate my yes to You. Open the doors of promises which are mine by way of faith. Thank You for strength over the enemy to tell him no and victory over the adversary to tell You yes.

In The Name of Jesus, Amen.

Day 6

God's Word For You Today:

HELL NO

The Mandate

Neither give place to the devil (Eph. 4:27, KJV).

The Message

The Apostle Paul is very keen and clear regarding his view of the devil. The word used for the devil in the passage is diabolos. It means a channel of confusion. The idea behind it suggests that wherever the devil is, there will always be confusion, darkness, division, separation, and an evil system of godlessness of some sort in place. When Paul teaches the Ephesian church not to give place to the devil, he is telling the believers in Ephesus to reject what hell has to offer because heaven has what's best.

The Mission

If you allow the devil to remain in his place of destruction, he will set up residence for the purpose of annihilation, to make sure your life ends in defeat and not victory. This is why it is so essential to fight the good fight of faith for everything the adversary thinks he can keep that belongs to you. If you give space to the devil, he will attempt to steal and destroy everything Jesus Christ died for you to have.

The Meditation

Lord, today I've come claiming anything and anybody that is rightfully mine by faith. I pray, Lord, You give me the strength it takes to remove any demonic construct by way of Your name and Your authority so that whatever is mine shall be mine forever.

In The Name of Jesus, Amen.

Day 7

God's Word For You Today:

WITH THE LORD OF HEAVEN, YOU GET EVERYTHING

The Mandate
Neither give place to the devil (Eph. 4:27, KJV).

The Message
With the Lord of heaven, you get everything heaven has to offer. The blessing of this passage is inherently seen in the fact that when you do not give place to the devil, you give space to the Lord. In short, you win the battle you're currently fighting. You overcome the obstacle that appears in your face, which looks insurmountable and seems unpassable. It means you are victorious despite the defeat that looms ominously about. You are a victor. You win in the end! With grace, gratitude should come from your heart to God's throne.

The Mission
Whenever heaven is on your side, hell stands no chance. Whenever God is on your side, the devil is no match. Whenever angels are before you and fighting for you, demons will never overtake you. Stand with the Lord and for God, and you will never give place to the devil.

The Meditation
Lord, I ask that You dispatch angels to my charge, so that no matter what I fight for, I fight from victory. Victory is mine because of You.

In The Name of Jesus, Amen.

PERMISSION GRANTED Week 6

This verse is one of the most powerful canonical truths expressed on the pages of Holy Writ. It not only empowers the Christian to resist the devil in every way, but it also releases God's permission for you to reject the lies the devil tells and accept the truths that come from God in His Word.

As you seek to put your faith into action this week, do so knowing God has blessed you with PERMISSION THAT HAS BEEN GRANTED! With this in mind, here is your faith function for the week. Purchase some sticky notes from a local store. Take a note and write down a verse that contains a Biblical promise given in scripture. For example, Psalms 121:1 "I will look to the hills from whence cometh my help, my help comes from the Lord which made heaven and earth." Repeat this process six times. This will give you a total of seven verses of scripture.

Please place these sticky notes on your bathroom mirror and recite them over your life for the next nine weeks every day.

The lies of the enemy cannot remain when the light of God's truth is known, lived, and declared.

Day 1
God's Word For You Today:
INSANITY MEANS………..

The Mandate

And when he came to himself, he said, How many hired servants of my father's have bread enough and to spare, and I perish with hunger (Luke 15:17, KJV).

The Message

This week's study passage is truly exciting. It's Luke 15, and it's the parable of lost things: the parable of the lost sheep, the lost coin, and the lost sons. In Luke 15:17, we gain a sense of what insanity means. The term originates from the Latin word *"insanus."* The prefix *"in"* means "without" and *"sanus"* suggests mental well-being. Thus, to be insane means to lose your mind, to forget where you've come from without recollection. It means doing the same thing and expecting different results. It means to be careless. It means to be thoughtless. It means to be crazy. It suggests that a person functions without using common sense. To be extremely risky with no real chance of reward. Insanity means to be without your mind, to be without wisdom, lacking sanity. It means to be short on reason. To expect a harvest from a place you have not planted a crop. To expect something for nothing. To have a disposition of entitlement without proof of ownership or a deed of trust. To speak without thinking. To be vain, ignoble, and incredulous. To be considered stupid, thoughtless, and empty-headed.

The Mission

If we were to be honest, there are times in life when insanity gets the best of all of us. It can best be seen when you make a promise to save some money but never change your spending habits. It occurs when you make a vow to lose weight but fail to change your eating habits. After gorging like a linebacker after a hard-fought game, you find yourself heavier on the scale. You have eaten fried fish, steak, loaded mashed potatoes with extra cheese, cookies, ice cream, and chips, and have the audacity to be shocked at your weight gain. People make resolutions with no intention of keeping them on January 1st of every year. Insanity emerges when we do the exact same things in the new year that were done in the old year, but somehow expect different results. Let's be transparent for a moment. There are times when we lose our minds. The great news about this week's devotional passage is this: with the Lord on your side, you can get your mind back!

The Meditation

Lord, thank You for my right mind. Give me Your thoughts that I might think of them. Lord, give me Your Word that I might obey it.

In The Name of Jesus, Amen.

Day 2

God's Word For You Today:

THERE ARE TIMES WHEN YOU LOSE YOUR MIND

The Mandate

And when he came to himself, he said, How many hired servants of my father's have bread enough and to spare, and I perish with hunger (Luke 15:17, KJV).

The Message

The prodigal son of the passage is usually a title given to the younger son within the story. He decides to ask his father for his inheritance while his father is still alive. The dad acquiesces and gives his youngest son his inheritance before he is ever buried. This prodigal son takes the resources, goes to a far country, and spends every dime with riotous living. He's in the pagan cities of Decapolis. He goes crazy spending his father's inheritance money on wild women, crazy parties, and a host of other things that are unmentionable for this devotional moment today. In short, he lost his mind. To make matters worse, he attaches himself to a pig farmer and ends up feeding pigs and eating the food they eat. But the scripture says that he came to himself. This notion of coming to oneself occurs when you realize insanity is present but can be cured. It takes place when you decide you want your mind back.

The Mission

When you gather yourself and realize that where you are is not where you want to be, it's then that you are on the right track. When you come to grips with the fact that God has a plan and purpose for your life, you are headed in the right direction. When you decide to place your life in the hands of your eternal Father and take action on that decision, it's then that the insanity stops, and sanity begins. It's where fear concludes and faith launches a brand new you for the future.

The Meditation

God, there have been moments I've negotiated right and wrong. There have been times I've just lost my mind. But today, I thank You for sanity and clarity. Heal my mind, Lord Jesus, so that I think with the mind of Christ.

In The Name of Jesus, Amen.

Day 3

God's Word For You Today:

THE BENEFIT OF ROCK BOTTOM

The Mandate

And when he came to himself, he said, How many hired servants of my father's have bread enough and to spare, and I perish with hunger (Luke 15:17, KJV).

The Message

The young man in the passage reaches a pig pen and realizes his father has servants who live better than he does at that moment. It should not go without mention that he doesn't make a change to gain his sanity back until he hits rock bottom. Rock bottom is the place that gives you the benefit of realizing that without God, you cannot do anything, but with God, you can have it all. Rock bottom is the place that God permits and allows you to hit from time to time, only to remind you He's the Rock at the bottom holding your whole life together. Without Him, your life falls apart.

The Mission

Insanity finds us all from time to time and leaves us in a place called rock bottom. The blessing of rock bottom is knowing that God, no matter how low life brings you, is always still there. He is the rock at the bottom! With this in mind, there comes a moment where you can see the benefit of rock bottom and move your life in faith to a place called grace that's higher than the top.

The Meditation

Eternal God, our Father, thank You for being the Rock that's always been there for me. I bless Your name today, and I give You glory for the mindset that I now have that says, If God be for me, I am not concerned about who or what is against me.

In The Name of Jesus, Amen.

Day 4

God's Word For You Today:

YOU KNOW BETTER, JUST DO BETTER

The Mandate
And when he came to himself, he said, How many hired servants of my father's have bread enough and to spare, and I perish with hunger (Luke 15:17, KJV).

The Message
There is a time in life when you know better but fail miserably at doing better. In many instances, failing to do better causes discomfort, temporary satisfaction, and moments of total frustration. However, there comes a moment when you know better and do better. This is the tension of this week's text. The prodigal son reaches a place where he knows better and decides to do better. He reaches this place when he realizes his mind is clear and his insanity has ended. He no longer thinks he can do one thing, repeat doing it, and get a different result. He now realizes that if he wants something different, he must do something greater to get it.

The Mission
Your insanity is cured when you realize the person who's really holding you back and holding you down is not just the enemy, it's the inner-me! It's not only the devil. It is you as well. God has given you permission to take your mind back. With this in mind, sanity happens with the next clear, conscious, and cognizant decision you make. Your real choices will make other decisions for you that will bless you in the end. It is in moments when you make sound decisions, you serve the adversary an eviction notice, and the power of Jesus Christ heals your mind.

The Meditation
Thank You, O God, for allowing me another chance not just to know better, but to do better. Lord, in places where I may be weak, You are my strength and my guidance so that doing better happens even in times where I'm too weak to produce it.

In The Name of Jesus, Amen.

Day 5

God's Word For You Today:

GET UP AND GO HOME

The Mandate

And when he came to himself, he said, How many hired servants of my father's have bread enough and to spare, and I perish with hunger (Luke 15:17, KJV).

The Message

There comes a time when sanity says, I need to go home. It happens when you realize the safest place on earth and the most secure place on the planet is your Eternal Father's house. Your Father's house is the place of God's covering, total forgiveness, divine provision, and spiritual protection. The young man in the passage reaches a place where he's so hungry that he is now on the verge of starvation. He realizes that staying where he is is harmful, but going home is safe.

The Mission

There are times in life when your insanity will only be cured when you get up and return to your Father's house. By this, I do not mean or suggest your paternal or biological father. I mean your eternal Father, who has all power, who sits in the sovereign reign of heaven, and who gave you life, health, and strength today. Rise and get back to God. Give God your hand and your heart, and He will order your steps and clear your mind.

The Meditation

Bless the Lord, O my soul, and all that's within me, bless His holy name. Thank You for allowing me to take my mind back, knowing that I'm clear enough to go home to the God who gave me my mind in the first place.

In The Name of Jesus, Amen.

Day 6
God's Word For You Today:
THERE ARE YELLOW RIBBONS EVERYWHERE

The Mandate

And when he came to himself, he said, How many hired servants of my father's have bread enough and to spare, and I perish with hunger (Luke 15:17, KJV).

The Message

The story was told of a young man who had sinned greatly in the eyes of his father. He was an athletic director in Florida. He had done very well and earned degrees, but lost his mind along the way. He became addicted to drugs and alcohol and was overcome with kleptomania. He ultimately lost his earthly possessions, including his wife, family, children, and job. In short, he hit rock bottom. He wrote his father a note of desperation and asked if he could return home. He asked his father for proof that if he were to be accepted, a yellow ribbon would be attached to the mailbox. That way, he would know it was safe for him to return home. He bought a bus ticket and made his way back to Florida. He arrived in Florida safely, got a taxi, and made his way to his father's house. As the cab drove down his father's street, he immediately began looking for a yellow ribbon near the mailbox. To his surprise, there was not just one ribbon around the mailbox; the mailbox was covered in yellow ribbons! But that's not all! There were ribbons attached to the bumper of the old car on the driveway that hadn't moved in years. More yellow ribbons were attached to every branch in the oak tree in the front yard. There were yellow ribbons everywhere! It was his father's way of saying, 'You are my son, and nothing will ever change that. Welcome home!'

The Mission

When you consider what the grace of God is like in relation to your mental capacities, you will understand that it's impossible to comprehend it all. However, consider this one empathic truth and download it onto your mental hard drive: God loves you and will never change His mind. When the enemy thinks your mind belongs to him, serve notice to the adversary that you are a purchased possession and your mind belongs to the Lord!

The Meditation

Lord Jesus, I know that Your mind is made up about me, and on this day, I want You to know my mind is made up about You. I desire You to lead me, save me, and bless me. Use me for Your glory.

In The Name of Jesus, Amen.

Day 7

God's Word For You Today:

GOD HAS NEVER CHANGED HIS MIND ABOUT YOU

The Mandate

And when he came to himself, he said, How many hired servants of my father's have bread enough and to spare, and I perish with hunger (Luke 15:17, KJV).

The Message

In our study passage for the week, we have come to know this young man in the story as the prodigal son, even though the word prodigal is not mentioned in the passage. The word "prodigal" means to be extravagant, to be overwhelmingly kind, considered extremely gracious, and even wasteful at times. In other words, the real prodigal in the story is not the son, but the father. The father in the story is so overwhelmingly kind, so extravagantly gracious, and even wasteful at times, that he never changes his mind about his son, no matter what condition he is in. When the story reaches its climax, the father sees his son coming home and runs to kiss him, puts a ring on his hand, a robe on his back, and shoes on his feet. The problem, however, is that he just left the pig pen. He didn't have time to shower before he got home, which means his father hugged him and loved him just as he was.

The Mission

Your life of insanity will conclude when you realize God loves you just like you are. The enemy's plans for your life and its destruction will conclude when you come to grips with the grace of God and His plan for your life. The blessing of having your insanity cured comes when you realize your eternal Father will never leave you in the condition that He found you. The grace of the moment is yours by divine design. Accept it. Use it and thank God for it!

The Meditation

Lord, thank You for my sanity. I want my mind back, and today, because of Your grace, I have it.

In The Name of Jesus, Amen.

PERMISSION GRANTED Week 7

Temporary insanity can happen to any Christian. This occurs when you do the same things, but expect different results. However, it is during moments of demonic attack against your mind that you must make a decision to take your mind back from the enemy. Worry, doubt, anxiety, stress, fear, unforgiveness, and resentment are just a few tricks of the adversary. In this stead, here is some news you can use: PERMISSION HAS BEEN GRANTED by God for you to have the mind of Christ (Phil. 2:5-11).

It's time to take your mind back! The Bible says, "faith comes by hearing and hearing by the Word of God" (Romans 10:17, KJV). With this in mind, what you hear is what you will ultimately become. In this stead, prepare for a spiritual mental download of God's Word. To make this happen, take a moment to download the Antioch App and explore the Bible feature. It is free, and the Bible will be read to you in the version of your choice. Once the application is on your device, commit to listening to God's Word for fifteen minutes every day. Your mind will change for the better because God's Word is always true and never fails to be effective.

What you hear is what you will become!

Day 1

God's Word For You Today:

THERE'S SOMETHING SINISTER TAKING PLACE

The Mandate

14 And when they were come to the multitude, there came to him a certain man, kneeling down to him, and saying, 15 Lord, have mercy on my son: for he is lunatic, and sore vexed: for ofttimes he falleth into the fire, and oft into the water. 16 And I brought him to thy disciples, and they could not cure him. 17 Then Jesus answered and said, O faithless and perverse generation, how long shall I be with you? how long shall I suffer you? bring him hither to me. 18 And Jesus rebuked the devil; and he departed out of him: and the child was cured from that very hour.

The Message

There comes a time when you have to tell the devil no! In a very practical sense, it is when you say to the devil hell no. When we consider the sinister, satanic attack taking place on the young man in this passage, it's enough for you to realize that the same devil attacking him attacks our sons as well. In our study passage for the week, a man takes his lunatic son, who often falls into the fire and the water, to the Lord's disciples, and they cannot cure him. Jesus shows up, and when He is finished with the young man, He rebukes the devil, and the evil one departs from him that very hour.

The Mission

There comes a time when we must become fed up with what we see the devil doing to young men in this country, in general, and young African American men in particular. Our sons are the leaders of our future. They are important enough for Jesus to die for, and if He is willing to die for them, we must convince and teach them to desire, by faith, to live for Him.

The Meditation

Lord, my son needs You. Bless him, lead him, guide him, and protect him, is my prayer.

In The Name of Jesus, Amen.

Day 2

God's Word For You Today:

CHURCH FOLKS DON'T SEEM TO BE TOO HELPFUL SOMETIMES

The Mandate

14 And when they were come to the multitude, there came to him a certain man, kneeling down to him, and saying, 15 Lord, have mercy on my son: for he is lunatic, and sore vexed: for ofttimes he falleth into the fire, and oft into the water. 16 And I brought him to thy disciples, and they could not cure him. 17 Then Jesus answered and said, O faithless and perverse generation, how long shall I be with you? how long shall I suffer you? bring him hither to me. 18 And Jesus rebuked the devil; and he departed out of him: and the child was cured from that very hour.

The Message

The most amazing thing takes place in this week's study passage. A nameless man, with his son, seeks help from the Lord's disciples. He thinks that because the disciples have been near Jesus, they too can help his son. There are times when Christians can be the most helpless people in the world, though, like the disciples in the passage, have been exposed to the greatest helper that time will ever know. In short, church folks don't seem to be particularly helpful at times.

The Mission

Before criticism mounts too harshly against the Lord's disciples for their inability to help the young man mentioned in the passage, there is at least one word of commendation to offer: at least they tried to help. Often, churches are found on the corners of communities around the country that have lost their energy and effort to try. Today is a great day to reclaim the sons of a family and community, but it will only happen when we decide to tell the devil no and at least try to save them.

The Meditation

Eternal God, my Father, I declare today, as I pray, that no young man that's been a part of my life will ever see a jail cell in his lifetime.

In The Name of Jesus, Amen.

Day 3
God's Word For You Today:
IT'S TOO DEEP TO SWIM IN AND TOO HOT TO HANDLE

The Mandate
14 And when they were come to the multitude, there came to him a certain man, kneeling down to him, and saying, 15 Lord, have mercy on my son: for he is lunatick, and sore vexed: for ofttimes he falleth into the fire, and oft into the water. 16 And I brought him to thy disciples, and they could not cure him. 17 Then Jesus answered and said, O faithless and perverse generation, how long shall I be with you? how long shall I suffer you? bring him hither to me. 18 And Jesus rebuked the devil; and he departed out of him: and the child was cured from that very hour.

The Message
When you reread today's passage, you will discover the young man who is a lunatic often falls into the fire and the water. A better way to interpret the passage would be to suggest he frequently gets himself into things that are too hot for him to handle and too deep for him to swim in. It's a beautiful portrait which suggests the demons within this young man are working on him to the point they often lead him astray.

The Mission
In almost every instance, the penal institutions of our country are filled with young men, in general, and young African American men, more specifically, who are there because they've been misled and misguided. They are in situations where trouble has found them, because they've been in spots that have been too hot for them to handle and too deep for them to swim in. The difference maker in their lives will be fathers like the one in the passage who refuse to let their sons lose.

The Meditation
Eternal God, our Father, my prayer for my life today is to make sure the young men who have been near me and are near me now know who You are. Show each of them day and night, moment by moment, month by month, and year by year just how wonderful You are. You alone are a Savior and a strong deliverer.

In The Name of Jesus, Amen.

Day 4

God's Word For You Today:

WHEN THE DEVIL HAS YOUR SON, THERE'S HELL IN YOUR HOUSE

The Mandate

14 And when they were come to the multitude, there came to him a certain man, kneeling down to him, and saying, 15 Lord, have mercy on my son: for he is lunatick, and sore vexed: for ofttimes he falleth into the fire, and oft into the water. 16 And I brought him to thy disciples, and they could not cure him. 17 Then Jesus answered and said, O faithless and perverse generation, how long shall I be with you? how long shall I suffer you? bring him hither to me. 18 And Jesus rebuked the devil; and he departed out of him: and the child was cured from that very hour.

The Message

One of the most interesting observations in this narrative for the week is the father's diagnosis of his son. When you read this passage carefully, it is clear that the young man in the text is demonically possessed. However, the father knows it is a demon attacking his son without a diagnosis of his problem being present. With this in mind, if the father has a son with a demon and the son lives in the father's house, there is hell at home because of the spiritual condition of his son.

The Mission

To say no to the devil is your permission, given by God, to reject what he has to offer. To let the devil have your son and have hell in your house is passive behavior that says, "I will allow it only because I do not know the power I have as a believer to resist it."

The Meditation

Spirit of the Living God, fall fresh on me and my house. Any spirit that is not like Yours, I resist it. I only welcome Your spirit, for in Your spirit, there is liberty, deliverance, freedom, and power. Thank You for my son's healing and the blessing of my home that is filled with a peace that only comes from heaven.

In The Name of Jesus, Amen.

Day 5

God's Word For You Today:

GET HIM TO JESUS

The Mandate

14 And when they were come to the multitude, there came to him a certain man, kneeling down to him, and saying, 15 Lord, have mercy on my son: for he is lunatick, and sore vexed: for ofttimes he falleth into the fire, and oft into the water. 16 And I brought him to thy disciples, and they could not cure him. 17 Then Jesus answered and said, O faithless and perverse generation, how long shall I be with you? how long shall I suffer you? bring him hither to me. 18 And Jesus rebuked the devil; and he departed out of him: and the child was cured from that very hour.

The Message

One of the most remarkable facts about the story we're studying for the week is that when the father realizes his son has a demon, he does something only a man of faith would do. He rises and takes his son to Jesus Christ. It's a sign and a signal that he knew only the Savior could heal what was going on in his son's life.

The Mission

When we, as believers, come to grips with the fact that God is still a strong deliverer and a mighty strong tower, we will pray more fervently for our sons. When we accept the fact, by faith, that God will always hear our prayers and fight for us, will we gain the fortitude necessary to take our sons back?

The Meditation

Like the man in the passage this week, I have come running to You, not just with my problems, my burdens, and my issues, but with those whom I care deeply for, like my son. Heal my son, bless my son, and deliver my son is my plea and prayer.

In The Name of Jesus, Amen.

Day 6

God's Word For You Today:

WHEN YOU TELL HELL NO, YOU TELL HEAVEN YES

The Mandate

14 And when they were come to the multitude, there came to him a certain man, kneeling down to him, and saying, 15 Lord, have mercy on my son: for he is lunatick, and sore vexed: for ofttimes he falleth into the fire, and oft into the water. 16 And I brought him to thy disciples, and they could not cure him. 17 Then Jesus answered and said, O faithless and perverse generation, how long shall I be with you? how long shall I suffer you? bring him hither to me. 18 And Jesus rebuked the devil; and he departed out of him: and the child was cured from that very hour.

The Message

The exciting part about this week's study passage is this: in the hour that you decided to tell hell no, in that same breath, you told heaven yes. To reject one is to accept the other openly. They do not open concurrently. Heaven and hell never coexist. It would be equal to light and dark coexisting. Wherever there is light, the darkness can never handle it, and light always wins. This father in the passage this week told his son 'no' by rushing him to the Lord Jesus. In response to being told no, heaven was released in his situation and circumstances.

The Mission

When heaven breaks loose, hell can no longer remain. In that moment, it's when God permits you to take back what the enemy thought he could keep.

The Meditation

O Lord, our Lord, how excellent is Thy name in all the earth. Today, as I pray, I thank You for giving me the authority to hold the faith that I have in You to bless the son that You have given me. Lord, bless and favor him is my prayer and plea.

In The Name of Jesus, Amen.

Day 7

God's Word For You Today:

IF YOU LET THE DEVIL HAVE HIM, HE WILL NEVER HAVE ANY HOPE

The Mandate

14 And when they were come to the multitude, there came to him a certain man, kneeling down to him, and saying, 15 Lord, have mercy on my son: for he is lunatick, and sore vexed: for ofttimes he falleth into the fire, and oft into the water. 16 And I brought him to thy disciples, and they could not cure him. 17 Then Jesus answered and said, O faithless and perverse generation, how long shall I be with you? how long shall I suffer you? bring him hither to me. 18 And Jesus rebuked the devil; and he departed out of him: and the child was cured from that very hour.

The Message

The hero in this week's story is not only Jesus Christ, who heals, but also the father who refused to let the devil have his son. He realizes that if he doesn't do something, his son will be eternally damned. You have to ask yourself, how did this father know that there was something wrong with his son's mind? It's because the same thing more than likely happened to the father when he was his son's age. Demonic figures sometimes attach themselves to families. What the father saw in his son was a part of who he used to be before he was set free.

The Mission

If you let the devil have your son, he will face a time in his life filled with hopelessness. However, if you declare and decree through prayer, faith, and belief that your son is free in Christ, he can and shall be free indeed.

The Meditation

Spirit of the Living God, Eternal God, our Father, God of ages past, and God of years to come, I submit to You right now, the one Sovereign Ruler of the universe, this petition: do not let satan have my son.

In The Name of Jesus, Amen.

PERMISSION GRANTED Week 8

Make no mistake about it, the devil desires to wipe our sons out. But, with faith in the Lord Jesus Christ, our sons will be favored, faithful, and make forward progress. In light of our study passage this week, your faith assignment today will be relatively simple. Personally contact a young man within the next seven days and whisper a word of prayer for him, encouraging him in the faith.

Your permission has been granted, and God has authorized this time of prayer for you and the young man you will be praying for.

Pray like the spiritual shackles of satanic affliction will fall off when you lift your son in prayer.

Day 1
God's Word For You Today:
MY DAUGHTER HAS NOT BEEN ACTING LIKE HERSELF LATELY

The Mandate

25 For a certain woman, whose young daughter had an unclean spirit, heard of him, and came and fell at his feet: 26 The woman was a Greek, a Syrophenician by nation; and she besought him that he would cast forth the devil out of her daughter. 27 But Jesus said unto her, Let the children first be filled: for it is not meet to take the children's bread, and to cast it unto the dogs. 28 And she answered and said unto him, Yes, Lord: yet the dogs under the table eat of the children's crumbs. 29 And he said unto her, For this saying go thy way; the devil is gone out of thy daughter. 30 And when she was come to her house, she found the devil gone out, and her daughter laid upon the bed.

The Message

As you read this week's story, take a moment and notice the desperation of the mother. She's a Syrophoenician woman, who is actually of Greek descent. She is viewed as a Gentile who can be likened to an animal, such as a dog. She gets to Jesus, and her mind is made up. She is not leaving until she gets what she's come for. In short, she's desperate. Her daughter has not been acting herself lately, and she knows something is wrong. The problem is a demon. The blessing is that this mother's resolve is straightforward: she refused to let the demons destroy her daughter's life. The woman in the passage makes a decision not to let the devil have her daughter.

The Mission

Some things will happen in the life of a young lady that only a mother or another woman of faith can truly understand. The idea about this suggests that when the devil shows up, and he will, there has to be a close enough bond between the one who is possessed and the party who knows what Jesus Christ can do to set the one in bondage free. This ensures the devil's grasp will not last.

The Meditation

Eternal God, our Father, be a strong tower around our daughters. Keep, hold, and bless them, is my prayer.

In The Name of Jesus, Amen.

Day 2

God's Word For You Today:

DEMONS NEVER PLAY FAIR

The Mandate

25 For a certain woman, whose young daughter had an unclean spirit, heard of him, and came and fell at his feet: 26 The woman was a Greek, a Syrophenician by nation; and she besought him that he would cast forth the devil out of her daughter. 27 But Jesus said unto her, Let the children first be filled: for it is not meet to take the children's bread, and to cast it unto the dogs. 28 And she answered and said unto him, Yes, Lord: yet the dogs under the table eat of the children's crumbs. 29 And he said unto her, For this saying go thy way; the devil is gone out of thy daughter. 30 And when she was come to her house, she found the devil gone out, and her daughter laid upon the bed.

The Message

Demons never play fair. When you read this passage during your study time for the week, you will discover that the demon attacks this woman's child. It's her daughter. You would think the devil would have attacked the mother, maybe attacked another adult. However, when demons are at their worst, they are dirty enough to attack our children. Deliverance, however, comes when a mother is desperate enough to do whatever it takes to set her daughter free.

The Mission

There are times when a young lady needs a maternal figure to help her rid herself of demons that are attacking her mind, her body, and her spirit. She must have a matriarch who can say, "I've been there, and I know what you're dealing with. If God can deliver me, He can do the same thing for you."

The Meditation

Lord Jesus, today I stand against anything that stands against our daughters. Thank You for being a strong deliverer, a life-changer, a game rearranger, and one who would bestow victory upon us in the face of defeat. Thank You for my daughter's healing.

In The Name of Jesus, Amen.

Day 3

God's Word For You Today:

FALL AT HIS FEET

The Mandate

25 For a certain woman, whose young daughter had an unclean spirit, heard of him, and came and fell at his feet: 26 The woman was a Greek, a Syrophenician by nation; and she besought him that he would cast forth the devil out of her daughter. 27 But Jesus said unto her, Let the children first be filled: for it is not meet to take the children's bread, and to cast it unto the dogs. 28 And she answered and said unto him, Yes, Lord: yet the dogs under the table eat of the children's crumbs. 29 And he said unto her, For this saying go thy way; the devil is gone out of thy daughter. 30 And when she was come to her house, she found the devil gone out, and her daughter laid upon the bed.

The Message

Take a moment and reread verse 25. As you reread it, look carefully at the last few words of the text. The words of the verse read, "and came and fell at his feet." This woman is in such a desperate way for the life of her daughter that she does the unthinkable. She falls at the feet of Jesus. It is a posture of worship. It is a place of intimate trust. It is a surrender which says, "if You don't help me, I will have no hope."

The Mission

The reason why so many of our daughters are bound is because there's no one falling at the foot of Jesus anymore. If we are to see deliverance and if we are to get our daughters back, it may become a requirement that some of us fall at His feet. With this in mind, believers must imitate the actions of the mother in this passage. Surrender to the Lord and refuse to leave His presence until healing and deliverance take place for those who need it most.

The Meditation

Eternal God, our Father, just as this woman from Syrophoenicia has fallen at Your feet, so do I. I bow my head, I bow my knee, and I say to You, Do not let the devil have my daughter.

In The Name of Jesus, Amen.

Day 4
God's Word For You Today:
PERSISTENCE PAYS BIG DIVIDENDS

The Mandate

25 For a certain woman, whose young daughter had an unclean spirit, heard of him, and came and fell at his feet: 26 The woman was a Greek, a Syrophenician by nation; and she besought him that he would cast forth the devil out of her daughter. 27 But Jesus said unto her, Let the children first be filled: for it is not meet to take the children's bread, and to cast it unto the dogs. 28 And she answered and said unto him, Yes, Lord: yet the dogs under the table eat of the children's crumbs. 29 And he said unto her, For this saying go thy way; the devil is gone out of thy daughter. 30 And when she was come to her house, she found the devil gone out, and her daughter laid upon the bed.

The Message

Persistent prayer always pays big dividends. Never stop praying when it seems like God is not moving. In today's lesson, one of the benefits of watching this Syrophoenician Greek woman come to the Lord is that she continues to request His power and strength, even after facing rejection from His disciples and silence from the Lord Himself. In other words, her mind is made up. She is not about to change her mind until her daughter has been set free. Her persistence makes a statement which says, "I'm not leaving until I get what I have come for!"

The Mission

There comes a moment when persistent prayer is the only answer that will yield divine deliverance. If you have a daughter who is under attack, it should be known that the devil is not going to allow her to walk away easily. It will require spiritual combat. It will take the actions of a bold believer who knows how to pray their way through. With this in mind, never forget God does answer the prayers of His children, and persistent prayer pays big dividends.

The Meditation

Lord Jesus, You've heard this prayer before, and today You will hear it again. Take Your hand and put it on my daughter's life. Do not let the evil one have her, but favor her in every possible way.

In The Name of Jesus, Amen.

Day 5
God's Word For You Today:
THE BLESSING FOUND IN A FEW CRUMBS

The Mandate

25 For a certain woman, whose young daughter had an unclean spirit, heard of him, and came and fell at his feet: 26 The woman was a Greek, a Syrophenician by nation; and she besought him that he would cast forth the devil out of her daughter. 27 But Jesus said unto her, Let the children first be filled: for it is not meet to take the children's bread, and to cast it unto the dogs. 28 And she answered and said unto him, Yes, Lord: yet the dogs under the table eat of the children's crumbs. 29 And he said unto her, For this saying go thy way; the devil is gone out of thy daughter. 30 And when she was come to her house, she found the devil gone out, and her daughter laid upon the bed.

The Message

When you look carefully at verse 27, it almost seems as if Jesus is being rude to this woman. Not only disrespectful, but downright wrong. This cannot be the case because Jesus is God wrapped in a body. Since God the Father is good, so is Jesus. However, what we do find in verse 27 is a cultural idiom which suggests the woman, who is Greek and from Syrophoenicia, is not a Jew. In this context, what's meant for the Jews was supposed to be only for those of Jewish descent. Her answer overwhelms our Lord by such a large degree when she says to the Lord, "Even children eat the crumbs that fall from their master's table. Even the crumbs that they throw at the dogs," she says. It was her way of saying this: I know that I am not a Jew, but even as a Greek, I need what You have to offer.

The Mission

There comes a blessing in knowing where your real healing will come from. Just the crumbs make a difference. Just knowing who He is, what He is, and what He can produce is enough for Him by faith to produce it.

The Meditation

Lord Jesus, my faith is in You. My mind is made up. I am desperately seeking Your strength and power for my daughter. Heal and mend her is my prayer.

In The Name of Jesus, Amen.

Day 6
God's Word For You Today:
FAITH IS ONE THING, CRAZY FAITH IS TOTALLY DIFFERENT

The Mandate

25 For a certain woman, whose young daughter had an unclean spirit, heard of him, and came and fell at his feet: 26 The woman was a Greek, a Syrophenician by nation; and she besought him that he would cast forth the devil out of her daughter. 27 But Jesus said unto her, Let the children first be filled: for it is not meet to take the children's bread, and to cast it unto the dogs. 28 And she answered and said unto him, Yes, Lord: yet the dogs under the table eat of the children's crumbs. 29 And he said unto her, For this saying go thy way; the devil is gone out of thy daughter. 30 And when she was come to her house, she found the devil gone out, and her daughter laid upon the bed.

The Message

This week has been a study of the faith of a desperate woman. Faith has degrees and dimensions. The Bible is clear. It is given to every man to have the measure of faith. Some believers have weak faith. The Greek term for weak faith is *oligopistos*. It means shaky faith. The term is agrarian and refers to the knees of a lamb at birth, which can barely walk. Then there are others who have faith that is not strong yet. There are those in the scriptures who have great faith. Great faith happens when you have the faith of Abraham, who leaves the Ur of the Chaldees to find the land he's never been to before, following a God that he cannot see. However, crazy faith happens when it seems like all hope is gone, when those closest to you have found reason to reject you, and God uses your life as a light to bless others. In short, crazy faith happens when you keep on believing when belief makes no sense.

The Mission

Thank God for a mother whose faith in Him never weakened or wavered, but remained steadfast. The mother in the passage came to Jesus for healing and was from the region of Syrophoenicia. Yet her faith was strong, her resilience was tenacious, and giving up was never an option. Her mind was made up, and her faith refused to let the enemy win.

The Meditation

Bless the Lord, O my soul, and all that is within me, bless His holy name. God, this day I say to You in prayer, I will not stop praying until You bless my daughter. I will not stop praying until every demon has been removed. In The Name of Jesus, Amen.

Day 7
God's Word For You Today:
DESPERATION LEADS TO DELIVERANCE FOR YOUR DAUGHTER

The Mandate

25 For a certain woman, whose young daughter had an unclean spirit, heard of him, and came and fell at his feet: 26 The woman was a Greek, a Syrophenician by nation; and she besought him that he would cast forth the devil out of her daughter. 27 But Jesus said unto her, Let the children first be filled: for it is not meet to take the children's bread, and to cast it unto the dogs. 28 And she answered and said unto him, Yes, Lord: yet the dogs under the table eat of the children's crumbs. 29 And he said unto her, For this saying go thy way; the devil is gone out of thy daughter. 30 And when she was come to her house, she found the devil gone out, and her daughter laid upon the bed.

The Message

Based on the outcome of this week's study passage, it is safe to conclude that desperation leads to deliverance. Had this mother not been desperate, with her mind made up, the rejection of the disciples and the silence of Jesus Christ would have turned her away. However, the story does not end with a desperate mother being turned away. It concludes with a woman who gets her daughter back from the devil.

The Mission

There are times when it feels like helping some of our daughters is a hopeless case. The great news of the day is that the same God who helped this woman in the passage is available to help those you love, too. With this in mind, the fight for our daughters must be spiritual, personal, and communal. In this stead, it will take more than just one of us to help her. It will take all of us. The battle will not be easy, but it will be well worth it because our daughters are the mothers of the generations to come.

The Meditation

I want to be honest with You, O God. There are times I become weary in my prayer life, and there are moments when I become tired in my well-doing. But today, O Lord, give me the strength of this woman in the passage who is relentlessly pursuing her Redeemer, knowing that what the Lord has for her daughter will never fail. God, I thank You for being a prayer answerer, and I thank You for putting our daughters back in our hands. In The Name of Jesus, Amen.

PERMISSION GRANTED Week 9

Our daughters are in danger. They are underpaid, undermined, and in some instances nearly undertaken. They are demonically attacked, socio-politically oppressed, and on the radar of satanic affliction. If the enemy had it his way, they would depart from the faith and become daughters of the devil. However, the enemy is a liar, the father of lies, and the source of lies.

In this vein, God has given you permission to take our daughters back from the adversary. In light of our study passage this week, the faith assignment will be relatively simple. Personally contact a young lady within the next seven days and whisper a word of prayer for her, encouraging her in the faith.

Your PERMISSION has been granted, and God has authorized this time of prayer for you and the young lady you will be praying for.

Pray like the spiritual shackles of satanic affliction will fall off when you lift your daughter in prayer.

Day 1
God's Word For You Today:
I WAS DOING SO GOOD AT FIRST

The Mandate
Now the serpent was more subtle than any beast of the field which the LORD God had made. And he said unto the woman, Yea, hath God said, Ye shall not eat of every tree of the garden? 2 And the woman said unto the serpent, We may eat of the fruit of the trees of the garden: 3 But of the fruit of the tree which is in the midst of the garden, God hath said, Ye shall not eat of it, neither shall ye touch it, lest ye die. 4 And the serpent said unto the woman, Ye shall not surely die: 5 For God doth know that in the day ye eat thereof, then your eyes shall be opened, and ye shall be as gods, knowing good and evil.

The Message
If you could walk through the Garden of Eden as recorded in the Bible, Genesis, Chapters 1, 2 & 3, you would discover that it was purely paradise. It was heaven on earth. It was a place where there was no sin. It was a place where there was no evil. It was a place where God would extend heaven here. When Adam and Eve were created, they were designed to be the very image of the true and living God. However, in Chapter 3, something catastrophic happens. Satan shows up in the form of a serpent, and nothing has been the same since. If Adam and Eve could testify, they would tell you, "Don't believe the lies that he's going to tell." Because when it all began, they would say to you, "I was doing so well at first."

The Mission
The enemy has been and remains a liar. If you are going to get your relationship with God back, you are going to have to put an end to believing the lies that the enemy has told you. Things like God doesn't care, God doesn't love you, the Lord is not here for you, and more than anything, you can do what God said not to do, and God is going to be okay with that.

The Meditation
Lord, I want my relationship with You to be closer than it's ever been before in my life right now.

In The Name of Jesus, Amen.

Day 2

God's Word For You Today:

SOMEHOW I GOT ALL MESSED UP

The Mandate

Now the serpent was more subtle than any beast of the field which the LORD God had made. And he said unto the woman, Yea, hath God said, Ye shall not eat of every tree of the garden? ² And the woman said unto the serpent, We may eat of the fruit of the trees of the garden: ³ But of the fruit of the tree which is in the midst of the garden, God hath said, Ye shall not eat of it, neither shall ye touch it, lest ye die. ⁴ And the serpent said unto the woman, Ye shall not surely die: ⁵ For God doth know that in the day ye eat thereof, then your eyes shall be opened, and ye shall be as gods, knowing good and evil.

The Message

Adam and Eve are now in the garden, and things are beautiful. The serpent is described in Chapter 3:1 as being more subtle than any beast of the field. The idea behind it was simply this: he was slick, sly, and sinister. From this moment in the garden, things go left and don't go right until we get to Calvary's cross. The idea behind this attack is very simple yet profound. The serpent embodies a spirit of evil. God does indeed make the body of the snake, but in Genesis, he is purely a spirit that says, "There is no way I'm going to let Adam and Eve enjoy the paradise they think they deserve." So, here is what he does: he lies, and from the lies he tells, everything gets all messed up.

The Mission

We serve a God who is best with a mess. The mess of the garden reminds us that the mercy of the Lord is what will meet our needs every time. Without His mercy, we will never be able to get out of the mess we've gotten ourselves into.

The Meditation

Have mercy on me, O God. In areas of my life that are a mess, I need more mercy right now.

In The Name of Jesus, Amen.

Day 3

God's Word For You Today:

HE'S BEEN A LIAR FROM THE VERY BEGINNING

The Mandate

Now the serpent was more subtle than any beast of the field which the LORD God had made. And he said unto the woman, Yea, hath God said, Ye shall not eat of every tree of the garden? ² And the woman said unto the serpent, We may eat of the fruit of the trees of the garden: ³ But of the fruit of the tree which is in the midst of the garden, God hath said, Ye shall not eat of it, neither shall ye touch it, lest ye die. ⁴ And the serpent said unto the woman, Ye shall not surely die: ⁵ For God doth know that in the day ye eat thereof, then your eyes shall be opened, and ye shall be as gods, knowing good and evil.

The Message

The Bible says that Satan is the father of lies. It's another way of saying that he is the source of lies, the course of lies, and the force of lies, that if there is a lie, he is somewhere at work in the midst. In other words, when you examine the lies of Genesis 3:4, where the serpent tells the woman, "You shall not surely die," from that lie until now, he's been the source of every lie. In other words, you may suggest that he's been a liar from the very beginning.

The Mission

When you desire a closer relationship with God, when you reach a place where you want your life with God to be strong, vibrant, intimate, and personal, the first thing you will have to do is put an end to the lies and open your heart to the truth. And here is the truth: He is God. It is He who hath made us, and not we ourselves. We are His people, the sheep of His pasture. We belong to Him, and God belongs to us.

The Meditation

O Lord, our Lord, my prayer and plea today before Your throne is this: give me a relationship with You that makes You happy. And it is precisely those things that I need.

In The Name of Jesus, Amen.

Day 4
God's Word For You Today:
TO HEAR A LIE IS BAD, TO BELIEVE IT IS EVEN WORSE

The Mandate

Now the serpent was more subtle than any beast of the field which the LORD God had made. And he said unto the woman, Yea, hath God said, Ye shall not eat of every tree of the garden? ²And the woman said unto the serpent, We may eat of the fruit of the trees of the garden: ³But of the fruit of the tree which is in the midst of the garden, God hath said, Ye shall not eat of it, neither shall ye touch it, lest ye die. ⁴And the serpent said unto the woman, Ye shall not surely die: ⁵For God doth know that in the day ye eat thereof, then your eyes shall be opened, and ye shall be as gods, knowing good and evil.

The Message

It's one thing to hear a lie. It's even worse to believe one. The serpent is lying to the woman; Eve is being deceived. Deception is the worst lie ever. It's because it's a lie, but with a bit of truth mixed in. The serpent is aware that he is lying when he says, "If you eat what the Lord told you not to eat, you'll be like gods." It's a partial truth, which makes it a whole lie. Besides, when you look carefully at Verse 5, you need to check the spelling. God is spelled with a small g-o-d-s and not a capital G-o-d-s. And most importantly, when you look at the sovereign God of the universe, there are no gods. There is only one, and it is Jesus Christ, Son of the living God.

The Mission

When there is a place in your life for the truth, make room for it, for the truth is so interconnected to who God is, until Jesus says openly, "I am the Way, the Truth, and the Life." The truth is what you build on. And knowing the truth reveals this one thing: just as you desire a closer relationship with God, God desires a closer relationship with you.

The Meditation

Unto Thee, O God, do I place my trust. Thankfully and joyfully, I come into Your presence, and today my request is simply this: help me hold Your hand and follow You in truth.

In The Name of Jesus, Amen.

Day 5
God's Word For You Today:
GOD DECIDED TO GIVE ME ANOTHER CHANCE

The Mandate

Now the serpent was more subtle than any beast of the field which the LORD God had made. And he said unto the woman, Yea, hath God said, Ye shall not eat of every tree of the garden? 2 And the woman said unto the serpent, We may eat of the fruit of the trees of the garden: 3 But of the fruit of the tree which is in the midst of the garden, God hath said, Ye shall not eat of it, neither shall ye touch it, lest ye die. 4 And the serpent said unto the woman, Ye shall not surely die: 5 For God doth know that in the day ye eat thereof, then your eyes shall be opened, and ye shall be as gods, knowing good and evil.

The Message

Take a moment and read all of Genesis 3. It's not a lengthy passage, so take a moment to do your devotional reading and read it all. Here is what you have to conclude: God is a God of another chance. You see, when the Lord comes walking through the garden in the cool of the day, He calls out to Adam and asks, "Adam, where art thou?" This is not a question of location. He's God, so He knows where Adam is located. It's a question about disposition and should be better referenced like this. "Why are you where you are? I left you to have dominion, and when I returned, I found you hiding." The good news about this narrative is this: the Lord does not take sin lightly. In fact, He makes the serpent crawl upon his belly from now until time is no more. He curses the earth with thorns and thistles. He makes the man work. He allows the woman to be in submission to her husband and to have pain in childbearing. He curses the earth. He curses the serpent. But He keeps the people. It was His way of saying, "I'm going to give you another chance."

The Mission

In what ways has God ever given you another chance? In what ways can you see God extending His love towards you to restore a relationship with you that says, "I'm going to look beyond your faults and see your needs"?

The Meditation

Spirit of God, thank You for giving a person like me a second chance, a third chance, and another chance. In The Name of Jesus, Amen.

Day 6

God's Word For You Today:

I LOVE HIM, BUT DOES HE STILL LOVE ME

The Mandate

Now the serpent was more subtle than any beast of the field which the LORD God had made. And he said unto the woman, Yea, hath God said, Ye shall not eat of every tree of the garden? ²And the woman said unto the serpent, We may eat of the fruit of the trees of the garden: ³But of the fruit of the tree which is in the midst of the garden, God hath said, Ye shall not eat of it, neither shall ye touch it, lest ye die. ⁴And the serpent said unto the woman, Ye shall not surely die: ⁵For God doth know that in the day ye eat thereof, then your eyes shall be opened, and ye shall be as gods, knowing good and evil.

The Message

One of the most profound messages given in the scriptures is this: God loves you. Nothing is more fundamental and primal than the clear and clarion voice of God, expressed from Genesis to Revelation regarding His pure, unearned, unmerited love for broken humanity. If this passage teaches us nothing else about the character of God, it puts on display this one part of His character that ought to live forever in the earth. God loves us, period.

The Mission

There are moments of human error that will make you think that you love God, but God no longer loves you. When there is a sin that has befallen you or an error of your way, it can make you feel unlovable. It can bring you to a place where you'll say, "I love Him, but does He still love me?" The affirmation in knowing that He still loves you is that He let you live despite the mistakes you've already made.

The Meditation

Jesus, I want to thank You that I'm still alive. It's a reminder that Your love still rests upon me. Now, Lord, let me build upon that love, a relationship that says, "I belong to You and You belong to me.

In The Name of Jesus, Amen.

Day 7

God's Word For You Today:

I WAS BLIND, BUT NOW I SEE-AMAZING GRACE

The Mandate

Now the serpent was more subtle than any beast of the field which the LORD God had made. And he said unto the woman, Yea, hath God said, Ye shall not eat of every tree of the garden? 2 And the woman said unto the serpent, We may eat of the fruit of the trees of the garden: 3 But of the fruit of the tree which is in the midst of the garden, God hath said, Ye shall not eat of it, neither shall ye touch it, lest ye die. 4 And the serpent said unto the woman, Ye shall not surely die: 5 For God doth know that in the day ye eat thereof, then your eyes shall be opened, and ye shall be as gods, knowing good and evil.

The Message

God had every right to destroy Adam and Eve and start completely over after they had sinned and did exactly what He said not to do. It was a perfect time to say, "Instead of me keeping these two flawed individuals, I will just let them die and start again." However, He does not do that. He has a point to prove, and the point He wants to prove is this: that His grace is real, that He is going to share the same grace that He shared with Adam and Eve in the garden with broken, flawed, marred, messed up people just like you.

The Mission

The beauty of one of the great hymns of the church says at its core, "I was blind, but now I see." After reading Genesis 3 and working your way through this week's study passage, you, too, should have a view of grace that says, "I know God loves me, and His grace is still amazing."

The Meditation

Thank You for loving me, Jesus. Thank You for never changing Your mind about me. Now, Lord, let me walk with You, talk with You, copy You, emulate You, simulate You, serve You, and worship You in spirit and in truth.

In The Name of Jesus, Amen.

PERMISSION GRANTED Week 10

Oftentimes, we boast about having a God who can do anything. However, for the sake of clarity, there are some things that God cannot do. One thing that He cannot do is make you love Him. He loves you, but He cannot make you love Him back. To be sure, one of the things that God sincerely desires is a personal relationship with you built on a love that is as solid as a rock.

With this in mind, what God wants you to do more than anything is for you to fall madly in love with Him based purely on who He is to you. It is here that we find our permission-granted assignment for the week. Take a moment and schedule an appointment to meet God. Establish a special place, a specific time, and ask the Lord to meet you there. The purpose of this meeting is to do one thing: to get closer to the Lord than you have ever been in your life.

Keep this in mind as you fulfill this assignment: God longs to be near you, and He is waiting anxiously for your undivided attention to be solely on Him.

Day 1

God's Word For You Today:

HE CAN'T TAKE YOUR SALVATION, BUT HE CAN STEAL YOUR JOY

The Mandate
My brethren, count it all joy when ye fall into divers temptations (James 1:2)

The Message
As we embrace the Epistle of James this week, it should be duly noted that the writer of this letter is the younger brother of Jesus Christ. Yet when James opens his letter, he does not refer to himself as the sibling of Jesus. He calls himself the servant of the Lord Jesus Christ. He lets us know in Verse 2 that if we do nothing else, we ought to count it all joy when we fall into the diverse temptations. It's a fundamental principle to know and believe that the devil cannot take your salvation, but he can steal your joy. Just because you are saved does not mean you know how to use the joy that Jesus provides for you every day. With this in mind, there comes a time when you want your joy back.

The Mission
The devil is indeed a thief. However, God is incredibly gracious. And to have joy is to know who Jesus Christ is and trust completely and wholly in His person, His promises, His prophecies, and His provisions.

The Meditation
Thank You for the joy that I have, Lord Jesus. Life is not always easy, and times can be challenging. However, I celebrate the fact that the joy I have is the joy You have given me.

In The Name of Jesus, Amen.

Day 2

God's Word For You Today:

JESUS AND JOY ARE TWO SIDES OF THE SAME COIN

The Mandate

My brethren, count it all joy when ye fall into divers temptations (James 1:2)

The Message

The word joy comes from the Greek word chara, C-H-A-R-A, and it is akin to, or closely related to, the word for grace, which is charis, C-H-A-R-I-S. When you look at these two terms side by side, you can tell that they are very closely related etymologically: chara and charis, joy and grace. The idea, as expressed in the passage by James, is to suggest that wherever Jesus is present, there is joy. And wherever there is joy, there is grace. In short, where there is grace, there should be gratitude. And wherever grace and gratitude abide, there will always be the goodness of Almighty God.

The Mission

There are times in your life when you should thank God for His goodness, expressed to us in the person of Jesus Christ. That alone will help restore the joy that you think you have lost and help you hold on to the joy that the enemy desires to steal.

The Meditation

Joy, O God, in You is what I need every moment to survive the attacks and assaults of the enemy. Hallelujah for a joy that is real and a peace that goes beyond human comprehension.

In The Name of Jesus, Amen.

Day 3

God's Word For You Today:

LEARN HOW TO FIGURE LIKE THE FATHER

The Mandate
My brethren, count it all joy when ye fall into divers temptations (James 1:2)

The Message
When you read the words "count it all joy" written in the passage, it makes you feel as if mathematics is going to be needed because the instructions are for you to count. The word "count" here in the Greek means to put your life in a balance, where you have good days in one part of your scale and tough days in the other. And when you get through counting it all out, your good days far outweigh your bad days. The idea is to conclude that because your good outweighs your bad, it's how God views your existence. Not bad days, but days where things were tough and he had to help; not just days of blessings, but sometimes days of testing that help produce the blessings yet to come. Days of tears, but those tears are used to help you have a sweeter joy.

The Mission
When you learn to figure like your father, you will see the faith of your father and learn to figure like Him.

The Meditation
Joy, O God, is simply knowing who You are for me. I desire more than anything, Lord, to have an unspeakable joy, not just because of what is going to happen, but based on things that have already happened that involved You in my life that made that moment the greater and the better.

In The Name of Jesus, Amen.

Day 4

God's Word For You Today:

HOW MANY TIMES HAVE YOU FALLEN

The Mandate

My brethren, count it all joy when ye fall into divers temptations (James 1:2)

The Message

The seed clause of our verse for the week is, "When you fall into the diverse temptations." This should not just be overlooked. It should be pulled upon because the secret to real joy is found here. The word "divers" comes from the Greek word "poikalos." It means different colors, like a black slip, a Blue Monday, or a red notice from work that says you're being terminated. These ideas of different colors suggest that trouble can come in various shades. The idea behind it is that you count when you fall, which makes you ask yourself, how many times have you fallen? How many ways have you fallen? In how many directions have you fallen? No one likes counting falls. We've learned to cover them up. But we're told to count them, because the more we count, the more we realize that every time we've fallen, the Lord was there to pick us up.

The Mission

Do not let the devil have your joy over the falls, miscues, and mess-ups of your human existence. Thank God for them, learn from them, and hold on to your joy, because the more you count, the better you will feel.

The Meditation

Thank You for a joy that will remain because I have enough mistakes in my past to keep me counting forever.

In The Name of Jesus, Amen.

Day 5

God's Word For You Today:

CAUGHT IN THE TEST TUBE

The Mandate
My brethren, count it all joy when ye fall into divers temptations (James 1:2)

The Message
The last word of Verse 2 is "temptations." It comes from a Greek word that means to put two elements in a test tube for the purpose of examination. The Greek word here is "pyrosmos," which means to continue examining a specimen until a reaction of some sort occurs. Divers' temptations, then, are different types of testing, a testing of your faith, a testing of no money, a testing of no way out, a testing of a death in the family, a testing of your wisdom. God permits tests, and though sometimes you will fail, God never fails you. This is where joy comes from. It comes from knowing that, though there have been moments of failed examinations, the Lord has always been faithful.

The Mission
When God is faithful to you, it should make you want to be more faithful to Him than you've ever been before. It should push you to a place where your joy comes in knowing that I will count it until it makes me happy. Because God had every right to give up on me, but He chose not to.

The Meditation
Thank You, O Lord, for not giving up on me when I was flawed in my relationship with You. Thank You for Your faithfulness and the joy that I currently have.

In The Name of Jesus, Amen.

Day 6

God's Word For You Today:

TO GET IT BACK MEANS TO COUNT IT WELL

The Mandate
My brethren, count it all joy when ye fall into divers temptations (James 1:2)

The Message
The conclusion of the matter from the Book of James 1:2 regarding joy is this: counting and joy are two elements of the Christian faith that belong together. In short, the more you count, the more joy you're going to have. If you fail to count, it will make joy remain aloof, remote, and obscure. In short, to get it back means to count it well. And if you count it well, you get it back.

The Mission
As you think about the times in your life where temptations got the best of you, when you consider the times when you knew better and failed miserably while God was watching, when you consider mistakes you've made based on decisions that felt good to you but were not best for you, the Bible concludes that this will give you more joy. Joy, then, is the recollection of mercy, the recollection and remembrance of God's love, the blessing of His forgiveness, and knowing well that He's never turned His back on you.

The Meditation
Lord, never let me fail to count the moments of personal misery I have had to endure based on mistakes I have made. Even those in which I had to forsake You to do it. Thank You for joy and thank You for Jesus.

In The Name of Jesus, Amen.

Day 7

God's Word For You Today:

THE JOY OF THE LORD IS YOUR STRENGTH

The Mandate
My brethren, count it all joy when ye fall into divers temptations (James 1:2)

The Message
As you peruse the pages of HolyWrit, you cannot help but come across verses and passages that deal with joy. For example, Psalms 30:5 declares that God doesn't stay angry long. But here is what we do know: weeping may endure for a night, but joy comes in the morning. The Bible tells us that the reason why people who cry have great joy is because Psalms 126:5 says, "They that sow in tears reap in joy. Nehemiah 8:11 declares for the reader that the joy of the Lord is our strength. And James 1:2 says that "My brethren, count it all joy when you fall in the divers temptations." When you conclude with all of these verses that are mentioned, you have to rest, rule, and remain that the way you get your joy back is to learn how to count.

The Mission
From now on, when life presses you, when things are torn, when life hurts, when there are tears and tares, remember to count it all joy. It's how joy is restored.

The Meditation
There are days, O God, when worry, frustration, agitation, and irritation get the best of me, but I will count my way through from now on.

In The Name of Jesus, Amen.

PERMISSION GRANTED Week 11

To have Jesus is to have joy. To know Jesus is to know joy. The reason for this is that Jesus is the source of joy, the force of joy, and the course of joy. The problem is that one of the first things the enemy seeks to steal from believers in every moment of our lives is our joy. At this very moment, you have to make a personal decision not to let the enemy steal or keep yours if he has it.

The great news of the day is that the Lord of heaven has granted you permission to take your joy back. According to James 1:2, the way a believer is to recover their joy is to "...count it all joy when you fall..." In short, joy is refreshed when you measure the times in your life when you have failed, faltered, and floundered miserably as a Christian. How does this restore your joy, you might ask? The answer is simple. In each moment you failed, God met you with His amazing, life-changing, life-transforming grace.

Take a sheet of paper and write down your worst mistakes you have ever made in your life. Include moments of current struggle. Be honest with yourself. Once your list is complete, look at it carefully and whisper a personal prayer of thanks to the Lord for His grace that has not let those mistakes destroy you. Write the word "GRACE" in giant letters across the sheet and rip it into as many pieces as you can. Put the shredded pieces into an empty water bottle and throw it all away.

Joy will return unspeakably!

Day 1

God's Word For You Today:

WORRY, ANXIETY, AND STRESS WILL KILL YOU DEAD

The Mandate

⁶ Be careful for nothing; but in every thing by prayer and supplication with thanksgiving let your requests be made known unto God. ⁷ And the peace of God, which passeth all understanding, shall keep your hearts and minds through Christ Jesus (Phil. 4:6-7, KJV).

The Message

Paul is writing to the Church of Philippi, and as he writes, he is careful to remind them of one watchword that ought to keep the church pressing her way forward, and that is that God's peace is our portion. This idea of peace suggests that God has a way of not moving a storm, but instead placing you in the eye of the hurricane, so that the peace God provides while the storm rages belongs to those who have been redeemed. Hear the words of Philippians 4:6-7 and read them this week over and over, because this week is the week where the madness stops. If you allow it to do so, worry, anxiety, and stress will kill you, but God's peace is what you have, and you can live with it every day.

The Mission

As a believer, you don't have to go looking for peace. The truth of the matter is that God's peace is found in His person. Therefore, to have Jesus is to have the peace of God with you. He connects you to the father without any interruption. You have peace if you have His person.

The Meditation

Thank You, Lord Jesus, for being the peace I've always needed, wanted, and desired.

In The Name of Jesus, Amen.

Day 2

God's Word For You Today:

TELL THE LORD ABOUT IT

The Mandate

6 Be careful for nothing; but in every thing by prayer and supplication with thanksgiving let your requests be made known unto God. 7 And the peace of God, which passeth all understanding, shall keep your hearts and minds through Christ Jesus (Phil. 4:6-7, KJV).

The Message

When you begin reading Philippians 4:6-7, you need to remember not to let your troubles trouble you. "Be careful for nothing" is better rendered as "you will have trouble, but don't let your troubles trouble you. Don't let your worries worry you. Don't let your problems be a problem for you. You must then ask yourself the question, why can Paul reach his conclusion? He then unloads a fundamental principle to practice for every believer on the earth: "But in everything, by prayer and supplication with thanksgiving that your request be made known unto God." It's a nice way of saying pray about it. A better translation is to tell the Lord about it. Tell God about what you are dealing with and what you are going through. That's the root of how to make the madness stop and regain your peace.

The Mission

All too often, we want to fix problems ourselves, deal with issues head-on, and end up with high blood pressure, stress-related illnesses, and hair that's falling out. This does not have to be the case. Tell the Lord about it, and let Him be God while you hold on to your joy and your peace.

The Meditation

There were times, Lord, I worried when I should trust. Please forgive me. Today, I'm deciding to tell You about it, leave it there, and function faithfully.

In The Name of Jesus, Amen.

Day 3

God's Word For You Today:

YOU CAN'T ORDER COLLARD GREENS FROM MCDONALD'S

The Mandate

6 Be careful for nothing; but in every thing by prayer and supplication with thanksgiving let your requests be made known unto God. 7 And the peace of God, which passeth all understanding, shall keep your hearts and minds through Christ Jesus (Phil. 4:6-7, KJV).

The Message

Notice in Verse 6 of our study passage for the week that we ought to have prayer and supplication. These two words, "prayer" and "supplication," though similar, are different. Prayer is the Greek word which means to make a list and give it to God. And supplication comes from the Greek word, which means to ask specifically for what's available. With this in mind, when you have prayer and supplication, you should pray and be specific based on what's available. Have you ever noticed that you can't order collard greens at McDonald's? It's because collard greens are not a menu option at McDonald's. You must order from the menu.

The Mission

The menu for those who believe consists of things like peace, joy, purpose, strength, direction, influence, forgiveness, mercy, and grace. These are always menu options for you to choose from.

The Meditation

Eternal God, our Father, I know what's on the menu, and right now, I have chosen to order things that You have promised to provide. Lord, You promised to be with us always. Today, I accept that promise as mine and live without the madness, knowing that my peace is in You.

In The Name of Jesus, Amen.

Day 4

God's Word For You Today:

GRATITUDE IS A GAME CHANGER

The Mandate

6 Be careful for nothing; but in every thing by prayer and supplication with thanksgiving let your requests be made known unto God. 7 And the peace of God, which passeth all understanding, shall keep your hearts and minds through Christ Jesus (Phil. 4:6-7, KJV).

The Message

When you read this study passage for the week carefully, you will notice that prayer and supplication are to be given with thanksgiving. In other words, you are to be thankful for what you've requested before God has even responded. Thanksgiving goes before the provision is made manifest. In this regard, thanksgiving is like the postage stamp on a parcel post. Years ago, I worked as a casual carrier for the United States Postal Service, and occasionally, I would have to return packages to the station that were marked as having insufficient postage. You see, the package was too heavy for the amount of money paid in postage, so they couldn't mail it. They had to return it. Many times, thanksgiving and gratitude are like that. When you tender a prayer to God, if you have a big package, then you may want to include a little more postage so that as God considers what you're requesting, the thanksgiving that's your postage payment is sufficient for the size of the package you're requesting for God to meet the need of.

The Mission

There is never a time when gratitude is a bad thing. In fact, gratitude is a response to God's grace, saying, 'Lord, I'm thankful for who You are, for what You provide, and for when You provide it.'

The Meditation

Lord, my peace rests in knowing that I can be thankful in every case, condition, and circumstance, as long as You are still on the throne.

In The Name of Jesus, Amen.

Day 5

God's Word For You Today:

I HAVE A REQUEST, PLEASE

The Mandate

6 Be careful for nothing; but in every thing by prayer and supplication with thanksgiving let your requests be made known unto God. 7 And the peace of God, which passeth all understanding, shall keep your hearts and minds through Christ Jesus (Phil. 4:6-7, KJV).

The Message

Prayer is not just asking God for things; it's communing with God, loving God, hearing God, obeying God, and also learning how to approach God in prayer. After all, you have to be careful how you approach a king. In that same light, when the king is your father, it does give you favor that others don't have. When Paul considers this favor, he says in the very last section of Verse 6, "Let your request be made known unto God." It's a wonderful privilege to know that God Himself receives your request. There are times when other people are just too busy. There were other times when people didn't consider your request because it was not important to them. But what's on your heart is always welcomed in God's hand. You can trust Him with it because He allows us to make our requests known to Him.

The Mission

Peace and prayer are your portion. Never forget that. As long as you can remember that God answers prayer, and from answered prayer comes a peace that says, 'I still have God, even if I have nothing else,' is the portion that will always give you the peace your heart longs to have.

The Meditation

Lord, thank You for my peace. Just knowing it's going to be all right because of who You are makes me glad about who I am.

In The Name of Jesus, Amen.

Day 6

God's Word For You Today:

IRENE SOUNDS LIKE A PRETTY GIRL'S NAME

The Mandate

6 Be careful for nothing; but in every thing by prayer and supplication with thanksgiving let your requests be made known unto God. 7 And the peace of God, which passeth all understanding, shall keep your hearts and minds through Christ Jesus (Phil. 4:6-7, KJV).

The Message

The word "peace," expressed in Verse 7, comes from the Greek word "Irene." Irene sounds like a pretty name for a girl. Irene is the Greek word for peace. The interesting thing about the term is that it is not used to describe the absence of trouble, chaos, confusion, or even warfare. Irene is a word that references the presence of God, not the absence of conflict. The idea behind it suggests that not having peace is not having God, but having peace is knowing that He is with you always. The shout of the moment is simply knowing that God will forever be with you. This is why this is the peace that goes beyond human comprehension.

The Mission

It makes no sense to live in madness when you have a master like ours. It makes no sense to lose peace when the peace of God is with you each day in the person of the Lord Jesus Christ by faith. So here are some simple instructions that will help you get your peace back. Hold on to God's unchanging hand, and remember that this too shall pass.

The Meditation

Thank You, Lord Jesus, for being my peace and my portion. And I say hallelujah for my peace and portion being wrapped in the body of a person. Bless Your name and thank You, Jesus.

In The Name of Jesus, Amen.

Day 7

God's Word For You Today:

NOT THE ABSENCE OF CRAZY, BUT THE PRESENCE OF CHRIST

The Mandate

6 Be careful for nothing; but in every thing by prayer and supplication with thanksgiving let your requests be made known unto God. 7 And the peace of God, which passeth all understanding, shall keep your hearts and minds through Christ Jesus (Phil. 4:6-7, KJV).

The Message

The peace of God, which goes beyond all understanding, that keeps our hearts and minds, literally means to build a fort around your mind, to build a fortress. Years ago, in first-century Judaism, the primary method of protecting a city was to build a wall around it. You can recall that from lessons like when Joshua led the march to Jericho, the walls fell down after they shouted. The wall was designed to protect what was inside and to keep bad things out. This is exactly what the peace of God does. It garrisons your heart and your mind, that God builds a fortress of protection around it made simply out of His care, His compassion, His consolation, and His love. It's a nice way of saying peace in God is not the absence of crazy, but the presence of Christ. As long as He's there, everything will always work out for your good.

The Mission

The cocky confidence of knowing that Christ is with you is a certainty you should live the rest of your life with. And this certainty will give you the peace that only His person can provide.

The Meditation

Bless the Lord, O my soul, and all that's within me, bless His holy name. Thank You today, Lord Jesus, for my peace that resides in You. I realize it is priceless, and I will treasure You and it until the day I meet You face to face.

In The Name of Jesus, Amen.

PERMISSION GRANTED Week 12

Our enemy specializes in chaos and confusion. Wherever the devil is in control, darkness, chaos, and confusion will be the result. The great news of this week is that you do not have to settle for what the enemy has to offer. God has granted you permission to take your peace back! God's peace is your portion.

In this stead, your faith assignment this week is to place all of your worries at the foot of God's throne and leave them there. This will require a release of your issues, concerns, worries, problems, fears, doubts, and heartaches to God. In this stead, here's your assignment. Choose a morning that you can spend with God. During your devotional time that morning, open your Bible and read the scriptures listed below. After each scripture reading, whisper a prayer of release to God, and you will discover that the peace of God has been with you the entire time.

Proverbs 3:5-6 ⁵ Trust in the LORD with all thine heart; and lean not unto thine own understanding. ⁶ In all thy ways acknowledge him, and he shall direct thy paths.

Psalms 56:3 What time I am afraid, I will trust in thee.

Isaiah 26:3 ³ Thou wilt keep him in perfect peace, whose mind is stayed on thee: because he trusteth in thee.

Jeremiah 17:7-8 ⁷ Blessed is the man that trusteth in the LORD, and whose hope the LORD is. ⁸ For he shall be as a tree planted by the waters, and that spreadeth out her roots by the river, and shall not see when heat cometh, but her leaf shall be green; and shall not be careful in the year of drought, neither shall cease from yielding fruit.

Psalms 9:10 ¹⁰ And they that know thy name will put their trust in thee: for thou, LORD, hast not forsaken them that seek thee.

Day 1

God's Word For You Today:

THE DEVIL HATES IT WHEN YOU WORSHIP THE REAL KING

The Mandate

Then saith Jesus unto him, Get thee hence, Satan: for it is written, Thou shalt worship the Lord thy God, and him only shalt thou serve (St. Matt. 4:10, KJV).

The Message

This week's study passage is inspiring. It's because Jesus, in Matthew 4, has been pressed into the wilderness to be tempted by the devil. We must begin this study by acknowledging that if the devil dares to tempt Jesus, he has no qualms about tempting any of us as well. The temptations end with the devil offering Jesus everything if he would bow to worship Him. "Worship," that's a word that you should hold dear because it precedes time and will continue to exist when time is no more. It is interesting to note, as we begin our study of this text for the week, that the devil hates it when you worship the real King.

The Mission

Worship of the one true and living God ought to be separated from everything else on earth, for He alone is worthy of our worship. There are times when we have other things and pulls that distract us from worship, but worship is the priority because worship is not just what we do; it is who we are.

The Meditation

Lord Jesus, I worship You in spirit and in truth for who You are in my life.

In The Name of Jesus, Amen.

Day 2

God's Word For You Today:

HERE'S THE REAL STORY

The Mandate

Then saith Jesus unto him, Get thee hence, Satan: for it is written, Thou shalt worship the Lord thy God, and him only shalt thou serve (St. Matt. 4:10, KJV).

The Message

To fully understand the true meaning of worship in this text, we must embrace the doctrine of the angelic conflict, which teaches us that before time began, God created angels to worship Him. He gave three angels specific assignments. He gave the angel Gabriel the assignment of the word. He gave the angel Michael the assignment of warfare. And He gave the angel Lucifer the assignment of worship. Lucifer became proud and thought that he should be worshiped, and God exposed him from heaven. And what God did to replace him was unbelievable. Instead of promoting another angel, He made a new species called humanity and gave us the right to worship Him. With this in mind, each time Satan looks at a person wrapped in flesh who would dare worship God, he becomes angry because we are those who took his place. We took his job. That's the real story.

The Mission

With this in mind, worship is not just what you do. Worship is who you are. And there is only one God worthy of the honor of your worship, and His name is Jesus Christ.

The Meditation

O Lord, my Lord, I will only worship You. I will not bow my knee to any other deity. I owe You my best, and I owe You my all.

In The Name of Jesus, Amen.

Day 3

God's Word For You Today:

DON'T TAKE THE DEAL BEHIND CURTAIN NUMBER THREE

The Mandate

Then saith Jesus unto him, Get thee hence, Satan: for it is written, Thou shalt worship the Lord thy God, and him only shalt thou serve (St. Matt. 4:10, KJV).

The Message

As you study Matthew 4, it would be beneficial to read Verses 1 through 10, rather than just Verse 10, which is our study passage for the week. It's because you will notice three temptations. The devil gives each temptation after Jesus has fasted 40 days and 40 nights. Like curtains up on The Price Is Right from years ago, you can pick which item you want from behind the curtain of your choosing. In this stead, remember this: don't take any deal from the devil. Don't take the deal behind the Curtain Number 3. It is because he offers Jesus the desire to worship him. Remember this: there is only one God, and Satan is not him. His name is another name greater than any name on earth, sweeter than any name we would ever hear pronounced, the name Jesus Christ.

The Mission

When you want your worship back, it should begin with prioritizing what worship is, and nothing should be more important than that moment. If you have time to wash your face, brush your teeth, get dressed, and make it to a meeting, there ought to be a set time that says, "This is my moment of worship with God."

The Meditation

Lord Jesus, I will never again let anything, anybody, any problem, or any circumstance rob me of my moment to worship You.

In The Name of Jesus, Amen.

Day 4

God's Word For You Today:

CLOSE ENOUGH TO KISS HIM

The Mandate

Then saith Jesus unto him, Get thee hence, Satan: for it is written, Thou shalt worship the Lord thy God, and him only shalt thou serve (St. Matt. 4:10, KJV).

The Message

The word "worship," expressed in Matthew 4:10, comes from an interesting word. The term used is "proscanao." It means to kiss. It was used during the era of Jesus Christ to reference a person kissing the ring of an emperor or a king. It was an outward sign of your obedience to the reverence, authority, and sovereignty of that leader. In this sense, we ought only to worship the Lord. Worship means to be close enough to kiss him. This is important because you cannot kiss Him from a distance. You have to be close enough in proximity to know who He is and to honor Him in that way. It reminds me of weddings and wedding days, when we celebrate the final vows and prayers. It is common and customary to hear the minister say, "You may kiss the bride." In that way, you have to be close enough to the bride for you to be able to kiss. You have to be close to the groom to see their eyes blink and to feel their breath upon you. In this stead, God says, Come close to me. Jesus makes it clear that He doesn't want to be close to anyone other than His Father.

The Mission

When it comes to worship, it should not be done from a distance, where your body is one place, but your mind is another. Get close to God.

The Meditation

Lord, I yearn to be close to You, closer than I've ever been. Even now, I say thank You, in a spiritual sense, for the closeness You have to me and me with You.

In The Name of Jesus, Amen.

Day 5

God's Word For You Today:

THE DEVIL DOESN'T LEAVE UNTIL YOU MAKE A DECISION

The Mandate

Then saith Jesus unto him, Get thee hence, Satan: for it is written, Thou shalt worship the Lord thy God, and him only shalt thou serve (St. Matt. 4:10, KJV).

The Message

It is interesting to note that after the first temptation, the devil returned. After temptation number two, the devil returned. But after temptation number three, the devil doesn't return. He leaves. The Scriptures show us that when Jesus is finished this moment with the devil, the Scripture in Verse 11 says, "Then the devil departed and the angels came and ministered unto him." This suggests that the devil doesn't leave until you decide on who you will worship. If you want to get the devil out of your face, you should choose to bow your knee, humble your heart, and submit your life to the one who is King of kings and Lord of lords.

The Mission

The devil will always seek to invade your space, to be in your face, and to get you to misplace who you worship and when you worship them. And when you worship Him, remember this and hold it steadfastly. There is one God, and He is the only One who should be worshiped. It is Him and Him alone that we should honor, and His name for us is Jesus Christ.

The Meditation

O Lord, how wonderful You are. I thank You even now, and I worship You, for my worship only belongs to You. You are worthy to be praised.

In The Name of Jesus, Amen.

Day 6

God's Word For You Today:

I SERVE NOT SO THAT I CAN BE SAVED, BUT BECAUSE I AM SAVED

The Mandate

Then saith Jesus unto him, Get thee hence, Satan: for it is written, Thou shalt worship the Lord thy God, and him only shalt thou serve (St. Matt. 4:10, KJV).

The Message

Pay close attention to the closing words of Jesus in Verse 10, "Thou shalt worship the Lord thy God and Him only shalt thou serve. In this light, I want you to remember that you do not serve so that you can be saved. You serve because you are saved. Worship, then, is a service that you render to God. Have you noticed that in most ecclesiastical settings, we refer to it as a worship service? It's because it's your job. It's what you should do. For you to negate the worship of the one true and living God says you've missed doing your job. You have your job sorely misconstrued if you have anything else in the place of the worship of the King of kings and our sovereign ruler of the universe.

The Mission

To get your worship back, reprioritize where worship belongs. Worship ought to be the centerpiece, and worship should be for you the raison d'être of the faith. Worship if you do nothing else for our God, is worthy of it.

The Meditation

Thank You, O God, for letting a person like me worship a God like You. My hands are those of a sinner, yet I've been converted. My heart is the heart of a person who knows wrong even when right is present. Thank You for allowing me to worship You.

In The Name of Jesus, Amen.

Day 7

God's Word For You Today:

TELL SATAN STAY OUT OF MY FACE

The Mandate

Then saith Jesus unto him, Get thee hence, Satan: for it is written, Thou shalt worship the Lord thy God, and him only shalt thou serve (St. Matt. 4:10, KJV).

The Message

When you hear Jesus say, "Get thee hence, Satan," it's another way of saying, "Stay out of my face." It has some attitude within it. It has some authority upon it. It suggests that moving Satan is simply a matter of volitional will. The ability to make a decision that says, "I know what I want and I know what I don't want, and most importantly, I know what I will not tolerate." With this in mind, to get your worship back, tell the devil to get out of your face. Move him from the place of priority and make a decision to place the worship, the honor, the obedience, and the glory back into a place that says, "God, this is reserved just for You."

The Mission

The Bible is a book that reveals to us what God is like and what worship of this sovereign Creator should be. Never get it mistaken. Worship is personal and private, yet there are times when expressions of worship are public. Unite with other believers in both cases, for He alone is worthy to be praised.

The Meditation

So, Lord, I bow my knee, I bow my head, I humble my life, and I admit that there is none like You. In this stead, O God, I worship You and You alone.

In The Name of Jesus, Amen.

<u>PERMISSION GRANTED Week 13</u>

The word *"worship"* in Greek is proskyneo, which means to kiss the ring of an emperor or King. In a spiritual sense, it means to honor God as your King of kings by living for Him every moment of the day. In a corporate sense, it means to pay homage to God in adoration, praise, and thanksgiving in a sacrificial way, saying to God, 'I love and trust you, no matter what my current circumstances may look like.'

With this in mind, permission has been granted for you to worship the Lord freely and without shame or embarrassment both privately and publicly. In this stead, the Bible provides believers with Hebrew forms of praise, in which He desires to be worshipped by His people in a corporate setting. With this at heart, make it your intent to honor the Lord using each of the methods that He desires from you as a worshipper.

<u>*Yadah*</u>
To lift the hands in praise

<u>*Todah*</u>
To thank God personally for what He has done for you

<u>*Barak*</u>
To kneel before the Lord

<u>*Shabach*</u>
To shout and thank God openly

<u>*Zamar*</u>
To celebrate God with music

<u>*Tehillah*</u>
To sing to God

<u>*Karar*</u>
To dance before the Lord

Day 1

God's Word For You Today:

HE WANTS YOUR FUTURE IN A COFFIN

The Mandate

4 Now when he had left speaking, he said unto Simon, Launch out into the deep, and let down your nets for a draught. 5 And Simon answering said unto him, Master, we have toiled all the night, and have taken nothing: nevertheless at thy word I will let down the net. 6 And when they had this done, they enclosed a great multitude of fishes: and their net brake. 7 And they beckoned unto their partners, which were in the other ship, that they should come and help them. And they came, and filled both the ships, so that they began to sink (St. Luke 5:4-7, KJV).

The Message

As we begin studying this week, I want you to realize that if the enemy could get you to become discouraged enough, he would put your future in a coffin. Simon Peter, in our story this week, has fished all night long and caught absolutely nothing. Jesus shows up with a large crowd, gets on Simon Peter's boat, and tells him, ' Push out, because I need to use your boat as a pulpit and the beautiful Sea of Galilee as a speaker system. ' He finishes His sermon. The Bible says He turns around in Verse 4, when He had finished His discourse, and told Simon, "Launch out into the deep and let down your nets for a big catch. Simon then responds, "Basically, listen, we've toiled all night. We've caught nothing. Nevertheless, I'll let out a net because you told me to." And when he did it, the net began to break with the fish, so much so that he had to get his other friends who were fishing to come and help him. Here is the bottom line to this week's story: if the enemy could do it, he would have you become so discouraged over your current condition. He would put your tomorrow in a coffin in the ground.

The Mission

Do not ever become so discouraged that your future seems to look bleak when troubles beset you.

The Meditation

Lord Jesus, favor my future. Grace me with the presence that comes from You that causes me to be victorious and productive. In The Name of Jesus, Amen.

Day 2

God's Word For You Today:

QUITTING HAPPENS MOST WHEN YOU'RE DISCOURAGED

The Mandate

⁴ Now when he had left speaking, he said unto Simon, Launch out into the deep, and let down your nets for a draught. ⁵ And Simon answering said unto him, Master, we have toiled all the night, and have taken nothing: nevertheless at thy word I will let down the net. ⁶ And when they had this done, they enclosed a great multitude of fishes: and their net brake. ⁷ And they beckoned unto their partners, which were in the other ship, that they should come and help them. And they came, and filled both the ships, so that they began to sink (St. Luke 5:4-7, KJV).

The Message

Discouragement occurs when you reach a point where you no longer want to continue doing something. This courage means the will to fight on. So when you become discouraged, you lose the will to fight on. Every high school graduate who drops out of school becomes discouraged at some point. A couple that heads to divorce court becomes discouraged and no longer wants to stay married. When you're fishing and have caught nothing all night, as is the story within our passage, you can become discouraged and want to quit. Therefore, quitting happens most when you are discouraged.

The Mission

The idea about your future suggests that if you quit now, you won't get a chance to see what tomorrow holds, and the only way to see what tomorrow holds is to hold on until tomorrow comes.

The Meditation

Eternal God, our Father, give me the strength to hold on, hold up, and hold out until my better day comes. I know You were there because You have never left me. Even now, O Lord, be my strength, be my portion, and be my courage.

In The Name of Jesus, Amen.

Day 3

God's Word For You Today:

HOLD ON, GOD'S NOT THROUGH WITH YOU JUST YET

The Mandate

4 Now when he had left speaking, he said unto Simon, Launch out into the deep, and let down your nets for a draught. 5 And Simon answering said unto him, Master, we have toiled all the night, and have taken nothing: nevertheless at thy word I will let down the net. 6 And when they had this done, they enclosed a great multitude of fishes: and their net brake. 7 And they beckoned unto their partners, which were in the other ship, that they should come and help them. And they came, and filled both the ships, so that they began to sink (St. Luke 5:4-7, KJV).

The Message

When you take a careful look at this entire narrative, beginning with Verse 1 and concluding with Verse 7, you'll discover that when Jesus steps in, it's when Peter is ready to step out. When the Lord decides to show up for Peter, it's when he has fished all night long, is exhausted, and says, "I've had enough." It's when Peter says he's had enough that Jesus says, ' Now let me show you what I'm working with. ' For one, it was a conclusion. But for the other, it was a point of commencement. For one, it was a place to stop. For the other, it was a new beginning. The irony of it is that if you can hold on, God's not through with you yet. You will live to testify to this when you thought it was through and over. God said, "Not just yet, because I'm not finished."

The Mission

The only way for you to miss the blessing of your future is not to be present. You must have something in you that makes you hold on until the Lord says, "And now I'm completed." Until that day, do not quit and do not become weary in your well doing.

The Meditation

Lord, there have been days, times, moments, and seasons I wanted to throw in the towel and walk off. Thank You for not letting me quit, and hallelujah for helping me hold on.

In The Name of Jesus, Amen.

Day 4

God's Word For You Today:

YOUR PAST WAS SHALLOW, BUT YOUR FUTURE WILL BE DEEP

The Mandate

⁴Now when he had left speaking, he said unto Simon, Launch out into the deep, and let down your nets for a draught. ⁵And Simon answering said unto him, Master, we have toiled all the night, and have taken nothing: nevertheless at thy word I will let down the net. ⁶And when they had this done, they enclosed a great multitude of fishes: and their net brake. ⁷And they beckoned unto their partners, which were in the other ship, that they should come and help them. And they came, and filled both the ships, so that they began to sink (St. Luke 5:4-7, KJV).

The Message

Notice, if you will, that the fishermen had been fishing in shallow water all night. We know that because the difference Jesus makes between the shallow water and the deep water deals with the position of the boat on the lake. Here's what He tells them: "I have a huge catch for you, but it's not going to be in the place where you have been fishing. It's going to be in deep water. In other words, your past was shallow, but your future will be deep. The idea behind it is that when it comes to places you've already been, mistakes you've already made, doors you've already seen open, those were moments where you were in the right place, but the water was shallow. But the deeper water will be deeper, where you will have to depend on God to navigate your circumstances. You'll have to rely on God for the provision and for the things that your human eye cannot see and your human hand cannot touch. It's what's yet to come that God says part of you and the rest of you belongs to Me.

The Mission

If you want what the Lord calls blessed, you will have to move from shallow conditions and circumstances to deeper things. In the shallow water, you can touch the bottom, but in the place where God is taking you, you'll have to trust Him to be your life preserver.

The Meditation

Lord, I trust You. So, Lord, take my future and do whatever makes You happy with it, and if You're happy, I promise to be pleased with the outcome. In The Name of Jesus, Amen.

Day 5

God's Word For You Today:

I WAS GONNA QUIT BUT I CHANGED MY MIND

The Mandate

4 Now when he had left speaking, he said unto Simon, Launch out into the deep, and let down your nets for a draught. 5 And Simon answering said unto him, Master, we have toiled all the night, and have taken nothing: nevertheless at thy word I will let down the net. 6 And when they had this done, they enclosed a great multitude of fishes: and their net brake. 7 And they beckoned unto their partners, which were in the other ship, that they should come and help them. And they came, and filled both the ships, so that they began to sink (St. Luke 5:4-7, KJV).

The Message

Notice, in verse 5 of our study passage, Peter's attitude shifts. In verses 1 through 4, Peter wants to quit. But right in the heart of verse 5, he decides to continue. The wording in the verse appears like this: "Nevertheless, at thy word, I will let down the net." It was as if he were saying to Jesus, 'I was going to quit, but I changed my mind.' I was going to stop, but something wouldn't let me. I was going to give up, but instead, I've decided to persevere. This decision, alone, defines what the rest of Peter's life will look like.

The Mission

One decision to continue in the midst of conditions that are not favorable can reshape the entire trajectory of your future. It is why it's a sin for you to quit too soon. There has to be something in you that says I'm too crazy to quit, and I'm too stubborn to give in.

The Meditation

Lord Jesus, I've come to You because I've decided to move on, no matter what life throws my way. I have chosen by faith to walk by faith, trust You, and live not by sight, but to depend entirely on You and You alone.

In The Name of Jesus, Amen.

Day 6

God's Word For You Today:

WHAT'S TO COME IS GOING TO CHANGE YOUR LIFE FOREVER

The Mandate

⁴Now when he had left speaking, he said unto Simon, Launch out into the deep, and let down your nets for a draught. ⁵And Simon answering said unto him, Master, we have toiled all the night, and have taken nothing: nevertheless at thy word I will let down the net. ⁶And when they had this done, they enclosed a great multitude of fishes: and their net brake. ⁷And they beckoned unto their partners, which were in the other ship, that they should come and help them. And they came, and filled both the ships, so that they began to sink (St. Luke 5:4-7, KJV).

The Message

The name Simon mentioned in our narrative today will be changed to Peter later on. The Lord Jesus Christ has plans for Peter. He knows who Simon is because Simon and Peter live at the same address. It's one man in one body. The difference is that Simon is the name of his past, but Peter is the name of his present and his future. The beautiful part about being near God, especially when life is tempestuous and you want to give up, is that God can see you right now, and you're not yet at the same time. And if you get a glimpse of what's not yet, it makes you want to hold on right now. Peter is about to discover that what's to come is going to change his life forever.

The Mission

There are moments in your life where you can see the favor, blessing, and benefit of simply knowing who Jesus is. God has a way of helping us to understand that He is a game changer, a life rearranger, and the blesser of our souls.

The Meditation

Spirit of the Living God, when I become discouraged, don't let my discouragement rob me of the courage to continue. Please, O God, in the name of Jesus, help me fight on, because I believe that what's to come is greater than what's been.

In The Name of Jesus, Amen.

Day 7

God's Word For You Today:

YOUR FUTURE HAS GOD'S FAVOR ALL OVER IT

The Mandate

⁴ Now when he had left speaking, he said unto Simon, Launch out into the deep, and let down your nets for a draught. ⁵ And Simon answering said unto him, Master, we have toiled all the night, and have taken nothing: nevertheless at thy word I will let down the net. ⁶ And when they had this done, they enclosed a great multitude of fishes: and their net brake. ⁷ And they beckoned unto their partners, which were in the other ship, that they should come and help them. And they came, and filled both the ships, so that they began to sink (St. Luke 5:4-7, KJV).

The Message

When you look at Verse 7 of this narrative, it should cause you to celebrate. It's because the one net that Peter let down had so many fish in the net that they began to break. It should be noted that what Peter was initially fishing for was sardines. A sardine in first-century Judaism was between two and maybe four inches long, but what he catches is a trout. It's why his net is starting to break. It's because the fish are a different caliber, a different kind. They're so heavy that they are breaking the net that he has. Your future has God's favor all over it. That's what this story is saying: stay with me, because what's ahead of you is best for you.

The Mission

There are times you will be tempted to go backwards and not move forward because you are more familiar with your past than you are with your future. However, don't let quitting be an option, and don't let going backwards make you think you have missed an opportunity. Go forward in the faith and watch the Lord favor you like never before.

The Meditation

Lord Jesus, I want to ask You right now for Your favor, for You to let Your hand rest upon me, to open doors I don't have keys to, and to bless me, O God, in ways I can't. Thank You for the blessing.

In The Name of Jesus, Amen.

PERMISSION GRANTED Week 14

If left to the enemy, your future would be completely destroyed. The devil would love to annihilate your tomorrow and kill you dead. But the Lord has His mighty hand of love, peace, grace, and mercy resting upon you. With this in mind, you have God's permission to take your future back. Please be mindful that tomorrow is promised to no one. However, if the Lord allows you to see it, what you want to do is make sure that the favor of the Lord marks your future.

To guarantee the favor of your future, ask the God of heaven and earth to order your steps according to His Word (Psalms 119:133). Make it your business not just to study God's Word each day, but to submit to its authority in every way.

With this in mind, your faith assignment for the week is to establish a Bible study regimen that takes place each day of your life for the rest of your life, starting today. Make sure that nothing ever impedes it. Study with the intent of not just knowing God's Word, but growing in the knowledge of His Word so that you become like the God who gave us His Word to begin with.

And remember, permission has been granted! Work by faith each day, and the results will be a future that rests in the hands of the Lord.

Day 1
God's Word For You Today:
THAT'S MINE

The Mandate
The thief cometh not, but to steal, and to kill, and to destroy: I am come that they might have life, and that they might have it more abundantly. (St. John 10:10, KJV).

The Message
So you've spent the last 15 weeks looking at things that God permits you to take back. Keep in mind, no one command says to take anything back from the devil. Yet the Lord makes it clear that He will permit you to lay your hands on things that the enemy thought he could keep. This week, as we conclude our time together, I welcome you to the Gospel of St. John 10:10, where Jesus declares and decrees that "The thief cometh not but for to steal and to kill and to destroy. But I am come that you might have life and have it more abundantly." It's just like saying, "My life belongs to God, and God gave it to me to live every day, and when I want my life back, I have a right to say, 'That is mine."

The Mission
When you decide to claim the life that is hidden in Christ for you by faith, you have a right to let the enemy know he has no right to the life that you live.

The Meditation
Thank You for the life You died for me to have. Thank You, Jesus, for the life You've given me every day. Without You, Lord, life is not worth living, but with You, each day gets sweeter as days go by.

In The Name of Jesus, Amen.

Day 2

God's Word For You Today:

THAT'S MINE TOO

The Mandate

The thief cometh not, but for to steal, and to kill, and to destroy: I am come that they might have life, and that they might have it more abundantly
(St. John 10:10, KJV).

The Message

The thief described in the passage is none other than the same one who is described in Genesis as a lying serpent. The thief is this beautiful depiction and description, vivid and full of life, of who the enemy is against those who believe. When you start to reclaim your life based on what is given in John 10:10, your life comes with things attached that will make you say not only, 'I want my life back,' but also, 'I want that too.' "I am come that they might have life, that they might have it more abundantly." The Greek here in the word "abundantly" means fat, abundant, overwhelming, beyond the curve, beyond the norm, one that God favors. And when you look at the things that God desires to do for you, it is not the minimum. It is not ordinary. It is beyond the ordinary to the extraordinary, which would make you say, "That's mine too."

The Mission

Even though the enemy has so many things that may belong to you, he does not have the permission from God to keep them, but you have God's permission to grab them. So grab that too.

The Meditation

Lord, I have decided not to let the devil have anything You died for me to keep. Thank You, Jesus, for victory in this capacity.

In The Name of Jesus, Amen.

Day 3

God's Word For You Today:

THIS ONE, THIS ONE, THIS ONE AND THAT ONE

The Mandate

The thief cometh not, but for to steal, and to kill, and to destroy: I am come that they might have life, and that they might have it more abundantly (St. John 10:10, KJV).

The Message

Abundant life for the believer is not uni-dimensional, meaning it's not just one thing. The truth of abundant life in Christ means that life takes on its multifaceted nature, with many dimensions. The blessings of the Lord are not just one blessing; they are numerous. They are innumerable. They are immeasurable. They are incalculable. It gives you the feeling of a child who's had something stolen, and they find out where it is, and they say, "Wait, I want this one, this one, this one, and that one." It's a way of saying, I'm not letting the enemy have anything that belongs to me. Abundant Living says joy is mine, peace is mine, love is mine, forgiveness is mine, strength is mine, valor is mine, salvation is mine. It's mine.

The Mission

When you come to grips with everything that God has died for you to have, you will never accept anything less than an abundant life that comes from the very throne room of God to your heart by faith.

The Meditation

Lord, I thank You for the abundant life I have in Jesus Christ that does not just consist of money, but a mercy and a master who meets my every need.

In The Name of Jesus, Amen.

Day 4

God's Word For You Today:

OH, I ALMOST FORGOT, THAT'S MINE

The Mandate

The thief cometh not, but for to steal, and to kill, and to destroy: I am come that they might have life, and that they might have it more abundantly (St. John 10:10, KJV).

The Message

The thief that's described in the passage has a three-dimensional cutting edge to his aim of destruction: steal, kill, destroy. The thief is described by what he steals. He steals what is not his because he doesn't have a right to it. He desires to kill because it's his nature. He desires to destroy because that's his aim and ambition. However, two aspects of John 10 should make you rejoice in terms of exegetical reappraisal. The first segment of the verse tells you what the thief is here to do, but the latter segment of the verse gives you what the Lord is here to provide. It begins with these words, "I am." Wait. I know we are going to rush to "I am come that they might have life." But before you get to "I am come," just deal with the fact that he is still the great I AM. And if He says it's coming, you have a right to lay hold of it in faith and claim it. It's like saying, "Yes, this is mine. That's mine. I want this, that, that, and hold on, I almost forgot that's mine too."

The Mission

The idea of abundance is what God has in mind when He thinks of you. We're not talking about a lack that is in your possession. We're talking about a provision that's in His. Oftentimes, you get confused when you look into your hand, but you will never become perplexed when you see what's in His hand for you.

The Meditation

I trust what's in Your hand for me because You have always provided for me. Thank You for the abundance that comes from Your hand to mine.

In The Name of Jesus, Amen.

Day 5

God's Word For You Today:

IT'S ALL MINE

The Mandate

The thief cometh not, but for to steal, and to kill, and to destroy: I am come that they might have life, and that they might have it more abundantly (St. John 10:10, KJV).

The Message

The celebration of John 10:10 finds itself in the fact that it's Jesus doing the talking, which means He has a right to inform you of what belongs to you because everything belongs to Him. The idea behind it is simply this: Jesus says it's all yours. The life in Christ, the justified sins, the sanctified present, the propitiation of your faults before God, being substituted by Him on the cross, it's all His. And because it's all His, you have a right in Christ to say it's all mine.

The Mission

The great news about the Lord Jesus Christ is that He never half does anything. He heals, saves, and delivers completely. He is going to take a broken person like you, and before He is finished, make a whole person to become like Him. The blessing of the Lord is never piecemealed, though it may come in portions. It meets your every need because it came from the right person.

The Meditation

Eternal God, our Father, thank You even now for being the God who never, ever fails at taking care of His own. And, Lord, thank You for taking care of me and providing for me the best life I would ever have, one that is in You that starts now and is eternal because of the faith.

In The Name of Jesus, Amen.

Day 6

God's Word For You Today:

MOST IMPORTANTLY, HE'S MINE

The Mandate
The thief cometh not, but for to steal, and to kill, and to destroy: I am come that they might have life, and that they might have it more abundantly (St. John 10:10, KJV).

The Message
The most important portion of abundant life is not the things that we think come in abundance, like abundant joy, abundant peace, or abundant provision. The essential thing is to realize that not only are all of those things mine, but most importantly, He is mine. By faith in the Lord Jesus Christ, when you have an abundant life in Him, you can say, "He's mine." Never forget this: Jesus Christ is heaven wrapped in a body. He became us to redeem us so that we might become like Him.

The Mission
As a disciple of Jesus Christ, the work of the Lord requires one who knows what abundant life feels like. One who knows that no amount of money can buy it. One who realizes that no check can write it. One who celebrates the fact that nothing compares to the finished work of Jesus Christ at the cross.

The Meditation
Lord, thank You for what we have in You, that comes to us from You, that without You we would not have.

In The Name of Jesus, Amen.

Day 7

God's Word For You Today:

LIVING LARGE IS LIVING FOR THE LORD

The Mandate
The thief cometh not, but for to steal, and to kill, and to destroy: I am come that they might have life, and that they might have it more abundantly (St. John 10:10, KJV).

The Message
As we conclude this study of those things that God gives us permission to take back, it should be noted that the real core meaning of St John 10:10 deals emphatically with the fact that living large is living for the Lord. Many people believe that living large is associated with material wealth and earthly possessions. However, living large is simply living for the Lord each moment of your life. For as you grow in the faith, it should be noted that nothing that you do not do for Christ is going to last. A better way of saying the same thing would be to say this: "Only what you do for Christ will last". It lasts to do what God has for you to do because in Him is your life. The scripture says, "In Him we live, move, and have our being...", which suggests that without Him, we have nothing. But with Him, we have it all.

The Mission
Live your life as a disciple of Jesus Christ, like that life is the only life that matters, because that's the life that will count the most.

The Meditation
Eternal God, our Father, at this very moment, I thank You for everything that You've allowed me to take back that the enemy thought he could keep. And today, Lord, I make a decision once again, to place my life in Your care, and to live for You, and to live largely enough that the world will see me and have to know the God I serve has favored me.

In The Name of Jesus, Amen.

PERMISSION GRANTED Week 15

God has abundance planned for all of His children. However, the enemy of our Lord's cross will do anything for you not to have it. Each week, you have been given a faith assignment based on the permission given by God to take back what the adversary thinks he can keep. As this book concludes, it is essential to ensure that your life is in the hands of the Lord. In short, the most important element you could ever take back to ensure that your life is hidden in Christ.

In this stead, our final permission granted faith assignment will be to check your spiritual birth certificate. To take your life back and place it in the hands of God. In short, make sure that you are saved, born-again, and covered by the blood of the crucified Lamb.

Here is your final assignment. Read the verses listed below. Read them slowly and carefully. If you are a believer who has actively practiced each one, it celebrates your salvation. If you are not certain, go to God in repentant prayer and ask Him for salvation through His only begotten Son, Jesus Christ! The only way to take your life back is to give the life that you have to Him!

(John 3:16) For God so loved the world, that he gave his only begotten Son, that whosoever believeth in him should not perish, but have everlasting life.

(Romans 3:23) For all have sinned, and come short of the glory of God;

(Romans 5:8) But God commendeth his love toward us, in that, while we were yet sinners, Christ died for us.

(Romans 6:23) For the wages of sin is death; but the gift of God is eternal life through Jesus Christ our Lord.

(Romans 10:9-10) That if thou shalt confess with thy mouth the Lord Jesus, and shalt believe in thine heart that God hath raised him from the dead, thou shalt be saved. [10] For with the heart man believeth unto righteousness; and with the mouth confession is made unto salvation.

(Acts 2:38) Then Peter said unto them, Repent, and be baptized every one of you in the name of Jesus Christ for the remission of sins, and ye shall receive the gift of the Holy Ghost.

(Ephesians 2:8-9) For by grace are ye saved through faith; and that not of yourselves: it is the gift of God: 9 Not of works, lest any man should boast.

(Romans 10:13) For whosoever shall call upon the name of the Lord shall be saved.

(Mark 16:16) He that believeth and is baptized shall be saved; but he that believeth not shall be damned.

PERMISSION GRANTED!!!

Other Books and Articles by John R. Adolph

I'm Changing the Game
Not Without A Fight
I'm Coming Out of This
Just Stick to the Script
Victorious Christian Living Volume I
Victorious Christian Living Volume II
Let Me Encourage You Volume I
Let Me Encourage You Volume II
The Him Book I
The Him Book II | The Anthology
Get Ready For Battle
Marriage Is For Losers
Celibacy Is For Fools
I Want Some Too
Victory: Ten FundAmen.tal Beliefs That Eradicate Defeat in the Life of a
Christian
Better Together
Based On A True Story
Back To The Table
Help Me Handle This
Necessary Changes

Articles-Zondervan Press

He Loves Me, He Loves Me, He Loves Me
I'm Certain That He Loves Me
His Love Made The Difference
God's Mind Is Made Up, He Loves You

Antioch Missionary Baptist Church
3920 W. Cardinal Drive Beaumont, TX 77705
Dr. John R. Adolph, Pastor
Website www.antiochbmt.org
FaceBook: Antioch Missionary Baptist Church
IG: @antiochbmt

Worship Service
Every Sunday at 8:00 am & 10:00 am
Virtual and Personal
Website: www.antiochbmt.org
YouTube: John R. Adolph Ministries LLC.

War Room Prayer Call
Every Wednesday at 7:00 am
YouTube: John R. Adolph Ministries LLC.

Bible Study
Every Thursday at 6:00 pm
Virtual and Personal
Website: www.antiochbmt.org
YouTube: John R. Adolph Ministries LLC.

John R. Adolph Ministries LLC.
The Message. The Ministry. The Man.
Website: www.jradolph.com
YouTube: John R. Adolph Ministries LLC.
FaceBook: John R. Adolph Ministries LLC.
IG: @iamjradolph

To purchase additional copies of this book or other books by Dr Adolph
or visit Amazon.com our bookstore website at:
www.advbookstore.com

Orlando, Florida, USA
"we bring dreams to life"™
www.advbookstore.com